WADSWORTH P⊦

MW00620634

ON

JESUS

Douglas Groothuis
Denver Seminary

THOMSON

WADSWORTH

Australia • Canada • Mexico • Singapore • Spain • United Kingdom • United States

ISBN-13: 978-0-534-58394-1
ISBN-10: 0-534-58394-6

**For more information about our
products, contact us at:
Thomson Learning Academic
Resource Center
1-800-423-0563**

**For permission to use material from
this text, contact us by:
Phone: 1-800-730-2214
Fax: 1-800-731-2215
Web: www.thomsonrights.com**

Asia
Thomson Learning
5 Shenton Way #01-01
UIC Building
Singapore 068808

Australia
Nelson Thomson Learning
102 Dodds Street
South Street
South Melbourne, Victoria 3205
Australia

Canada
Nelson Thomson Learning
1120 Birchmount Road
Toronto, Ontario M1K 5G4
Canada

Europe/Middle East/South Africa
Thomson Learning
High Holborn House
50-51 Bedford Row
London WC1R 4LR
United Kingdom

Latin America
Thomson Learning
Seneca, 53
Colonia Polanco
11560 Mexico D.F.
Mexico

Spain
Paraninfo Thomson Learning
Calle/Magallanes, 25
28015 Madrid, Spain

Contents

Preface

Why another book on Jesus when we are flooded with new and controversial books about him? *On Jesus* investigates Jesus' *philosophical claims*—his worldview and his methods of argument. This dimension of Jesus is often strangely missed in the literature.

On Jesus is not a "life of Christ" or a history of Christianity. Neither does it advance a novel perspective on Jesus or focus on what others have said about him. Rather, it investigates Jesus as a *bona fide* philosopher, whatever else he may be. This claim is disputed, so I defend it in chapter one. I center on the teachings of Jesus as recorded in the four Gospels, although I also give several references to pertinent Hebrew Scriptures and the rest of the New Testament. (Many of the accounts of Jesus' life are related in more than one Gospel. Rather than list all the references to one teaching or event, I typically cite only one account. All biblical citations are from the New International Version Inclusive Language Edition.) Since there are other possible source materials for Jesus outside the Gospels (such as Gnostic writings), and because many question the historical reliability of the Gospels, I offer a chapter on the historical trustworthiness of the canonical Gospels. I arrange the discussions on Jesus according to philosophical and ethical categories instead of those used by biblical scholars and theologians. I also relate Jesus' worldview to some perennial and contemporary debates in philosophy. Lastly, I discuss Jesus' controversial claims about himself and how one might rationally assess them.

My thanks go to Dr. Daniel Kolak, who kindly suggested I write this book. I appreciate the comments of Dr. James Sire, Dr. David Werther, Dr. Gordon Lewis, and Dr. Craig Blomberg. My deepest thanks go to Rebecca Merrill Groothuis, my wife, who edited significantly every chapter. To her I dedicate this book.

i

1

Was Jesus a Philosopher?

This question was posed by the moderator at an early Republication presidential debate in 1999: "Who is your favorite political philosopher?" George W. Bush surprised, if not stunned, his fellow candidates, moderator, and audience when he tersely declared, "Jesus Christ, because he changed my life."

At the philosophical level, we might say candidate Bush dropped the ball. He gave a religious or devotional justification for his choice of Jesus as favorite philosopher instead of stipulating just what it was about Jesus *as a philosopher* that he valued above other philosophers.

The responses to Bush's one-liner ranged all over the political map. Was his response just shameless, pious posturing? Or was it a sincere and disarmingly modest confession—or just inappropriate in that setting however sincere it may have been? In any event, Bush's clipped but controversial response raises a deeper question largely if not entirely avoided in the popular press: Was Jesus—whatever else he may have been—a *bona fide* philosopher? If the answer is Yes, several other engaging sorts of questions emerge: What kind of philosopher was he? What did he believe and why? How does his philosophy relate to that of other philosophers? Does his philosophizing have anything to contribute to contemporary philosophical debates? Further, just what is a philosopher anyway?

Jesus and the Philosophers

Jesus remains a potent symbol for influencing opinion, political or otherwise. Some teenagers wear bracelets with the initials WWJD, which stands for "What would Jesus do?" This reveals that they regard

1

him as a moral exemplar, the ideal ethical agent, who should be emulated because of his character and insight. The same perspective is expressed in the classic medieval text on spiritual devotion, *The Imitation of Christ*, by Thomas á Kempis.

Some today claim to know Jesus' essential philosophy and use it for marshalling mass opinion. People for the Equal Treatment of Animals (PETA) launched a campaign in 2000 claiming that Jesus was a vegetarian. One of their advertisements features an iconic depiction of Jesus surrounded not by a nimbus, but by an orange slice. It reads: "Be merciful. Go vegetarian." Claiming that an ancient Jew who celebrated Passover was a vegetarian is highly implausible. Nevertheless, the campaign shows the importance people place on Jesus' outlook.

No one can sanely question the global, historical, and perennial influence of Jesus of Nazareth in every area of human endeavor. In a work limited to Jesus' influence in Western culture, the esteemed historian Jaroslav Pelikan wrote:

> Regardless of what anyone may personally think or believe about him, Jesus of Nazareth has been the dominant figure in the history of Western culture for almost twenty centuries. If it were possible, with some sort of super magnet, to pull out of that history every scrap of metal bearing at least a trace of his name, how much would be left?[1]

In the last several decades the most explosive growth of Christian belief has occurred not in the West, but in the developing world. Moreover, Jesus' influence has never been confined to the West. He was, to steal a term from Hegel, a "world-historical" figure, whose life continues to radiate and resonate worldwide.

But none of this directly answers the question before us: Was Jesus a philosopher? Most reference books in philosophy apparently think that Jesus was not a philosopher, given the lack of references to him. For example, *The Encyclopedia of Philosophy* (1967), long a standard reference work, has no entry under "Jesus" or "Christ." The newer and well-respected *Routledge Encyclopedia of Philosophy* (1998) has no entry for "Jesus" or "Christ," but includes one on "Buddha." Even the recent resurgence in Christian philosophy, evidenced by the size and influence of the Society of Christian Philosophers, seems to have done little to counter these conspicuous omissions.[2] Karl Jaspers includes Jesus (along with Socrates, Buddha and Confucius) in the first slim volume of *The Great Philosophers*

(1957), but this is rare. As we will see, Jaspers did not esteem Jesus as a philosopher in the classical sense.

Jesus certainly influenced philosophers and thinkers of all kinds (Augustine, Anselm, Aquinas, Pascal, Kierkegaard, etc.), and countless thinkers have philosophized about him (how could he be both divine and human?) but this, in itself, does not make Jesus a philosopher. The philosopher Augustine was very influenced by his pious mother Monica, but that does not make her a philosopher.

One's religious commitments do not necessarily answer this question *a priori*. One may worship Jesus as God Incarnate yet be puzzled or even offended at the notion that he was a philosopher. "Isn't philosophy something the Apostle Paul warned against?" one might object, based on a certain reading of the second chapter of Colossians (verse eight), which warns of "hollow and deceptive philosophy."

But even those with no fear of philosophy *per se* may demur at defining Jesus as a philosopher. In a move unlike virtually all other recent histories of philosophy, the Protestant philosopher Gordon Clark devotes several pages to Jesus' thought in his once-popular history of philosophy, *Thales to Dewey* (1957). Clark denies that Jesus was "a naïve, nontheological teacher of simple morality," as some have affirmed. But Clark asserts that although Jesus had a developed monotheistic theology, his importance lies not in what he taught, but in what he did—particularly his death—and in his claim to be God incarnate. For Clark, Jesus as a teacher (or philosopher) takes a back seat to Jesus as crucified and risen savior. Clark seems worried that if one emphasizes the teaching of Jesus this might demote him to a mere moralist, stripping him of his supernatural credentials. [3]

Conversely, contemporary Christian philosopher Dallas Willard insists that Jesus was the most intelligent person who ever lived. He laments that so many fail to take note of this and instead view Jesus as "a mere icon, a wraithlike semblance of a man, fit for the role of sacrificial lamb or alienated social critic, perhaps, but little more." [4] For Willard, a religious commitment to Jesus entails a certain view of his intellectual abilities: "'Jesus is Lord' can mean little in practice for anyone who has to hesitate before saying, 'Jesus is smart.' He is not just nice, he is brilliant." [5] Willard certainly does not shy away from deeming Jesus a philosopher.

It seems that the presence or absence of Christian faith does not automatically answer the question of whether Jesus was a philosopher. We must delve deeper into the matter by attending to Jesus' statements in the Gospels.

Jews, Greeks, and Philosophers

Some have excluded Jesus from the ranks of the philosophers simply because he happened to be an ancient Jew, and not a Greek. Historian Humphrey Carpenter entitles a section of his short book on Jesus, "Jew, Not Philosopher." His assessment trades on the well-worn notion that Jews never developed philosophy because they, unlike the venerable Greeks, were too theological, and, therefore, not speculative. Reason was not their tool of enlightenment. Jews were called to believe and obey a higher authority, which they rarely questioned and never investigated in any truly philosophical fashion.

Carpenter asks if Jesus' teachings would appear remarkable when contrasted with those of Plato and Aristotle. His answer is that "such a comparison is meaningless."[6] This conclusion was not reached because of their different ideas about humanity and the good life, but because of their different approach to knowledge. Plato and Aristotle constructed "elaborate philosophical models of man and the world, from which they deduced ethical conclusions." But Jesus supposedly lacked such a system. His *modus operandi* was "inspirational," not discursive or systematic. Jesus was unsystematic to the point that he had "no concern with consistency in his teaching."[7] Although Carpenter allows that philosophers may glean insights from Jesus, "Jesus himself...was no philosopher; his mind was characteristically Jewish."[8]

Carpenter's position is puzzling. First, he seems to identify philosophy *per se* with the Greek philosophy of Plato and Aristotle. While these giants are paradigmatic philosophers, a thinker need not resemble them in every way to be a philosopher. Nietzsche, for instance, is deemed a philosopher by nearly everyone; yet he was not systematic and took pride in that fact. Moreover, he often wrote in parables, stories and aphorisms—methods used by Jesus himself.

Carpenter's criteria for being a philosopher would appear to shut out Socrates, a character vital to the philosophy of Plato and all subsequent philosophy. Socrates built no system but engaged in protracted dialectic with a host of interlocutors. He was a gadfly and a midwife, not a builder of an intellectual edifice. Worse yet, like Jesus, he wrote nothing. What we know of him is preserved in other's writings, principally Plato's. This is another parallel to Jesus, whose words are recorded by others in the Gospels. Moreover, Socrates himself operated in the "inspirational" mode when seized by his "daimonion," an unphilosophical thing to do, according to Carpenter.

Interestingly, in his discussion of Jesus' approach to the Jewish Law, Carpenter notes that Jesus did not endorse blind obedience to the Law, "but the kind of *reasoning* obedience which considers why God has given some particular commandment to men."[9] Carpenter further maintains that if Jesus thought in terms of conscience, "he would presumably have regarded it as the will of God expressing itself clearly in human *reason*."[10] Jesus, according to Carpenter, uses reason in his understanding of God, the Law, and the proper human response to God—yet he is somehow not a philosopher because he was non-rational and unsystematic. This looks inconsistent.

What is a Philosopher?

These reflections show that we cannot proceed further in answering our question, "Was Jesus a philosopher?" without thinking more clearly about the term "philosopher." What qualifies someone as a philosopher? We can certainly point to uncontroversial specimens, such as Plato and Aristotle. This is an ostensive definition: we pick out a referent that fits the category. But what of harder cases, such as Jesus? Of course, philosophers philosophize, but not everyone who philosophizes is a philosopher, just as not everyone who works on an automobile is a mechanic. We think of most philosophers as intelligent, but not all the intelligent are philosophers. Many individuals' intelligence may not be invested primarily in philosophy. Neither can we limit the philosophers to those who are formal academics, those who hold professorships in philosophy. Some philosophers, such as Hume, Spinoza, and Pascal, have lacked institutional affiliation, but not philosophical credentials.

Rather than chase down further definitional dead ends, I propose that the necessary and sufficient conditions for being a philosopher (whether good or bad, major or minor, employed or unemployed) are a strong and lived-out inclination to pursue truth about philosophical matters through the rigorous use of human reasoning, and to do so with some intellectual facility. The last proviso is added to rule out those who may fancy themselves philosophers but cannot philosophize well enough to merit the title. Even a bad philosopher must be able to philosophize in some recognizable sense. By "philosophical matters" I mean the enduring questions of life's meaning, purpose, and value as they relate to all the major divisions of philosophy (primarily epistemology, metaphysics, and ethics).

What makes a question philosophical may be highlighted by the following: To explain the physical basis of vision is not, in itself, a philosophical matter, but a scientific one regarding physics and physiology. But to ask whether vision allows us to know the external world as it is in itself is a philosophical question regarding realism and nonrealism. Likewise, to ask whether a personal agent may be immaterial (such as God or an angel) is a philosophical question.

Yet one may speak to life's meaning, purpose, and value in a nonphilosophical manner—by merely issuing assertions or by simply declaring divine judgments with no further discussion. A philosophical approach to these matters, on the contrary, explores the logic or rationale of various claims about reality; it sniffs out intellectual presuppositions and implications; it ponders possibilities and weighs their rational credibility.

Therefore, the work of a philosopher need not include system-building, nor need it exclude religious authority or even divine inspiration so long as this perspective does not preclude rational argumentation. Being a philosopher .requires a certain orientation to knowledge, a willingness to argue and debate logically, and to do so with some proficiency. On this account, was Jesus a philosopher?

Was Jesus a Philosopher?

Despite Jesus' inclusion in the *Great Philosophers* series, Karl Jaspers discounts Jesus as a traditional philosopher because he "preaches not knowledge, but faith," and he "shows little concern for logical consistency."[11] Jesus was a prophet heralding the end of the world and calling people to a new order of life in light of this immanent urgency, "not a philosopher who reflects methodically and systematically orders his ideas."[12] He cannot take a "place in the history of philosophy with any rational positions."[13] However, if Jesus' lack of concern for knowledge ordered into a system disqualifies him as a philosopher, it should also exclude Socrates, Nietzsche, and Wittgenstein, who built no systems.

Inconsistency in philosophy, or elsewhere, is no virtue, but a vice. If one affirms A and non-A in the same way and in the same respect, one has affirmed nothing—except a classic defect in reasoning (violating the law of noncontradiction). Nevertheless, some philosophers have viewed consistency with some skepticism, thinking that reality is too complex or opaque for such stipulations. That may have rendered them bad philosophers, but it does not disqualify them from the ranks entirely. Besides, philosophers who explicitly prize consistency (the vast majority) sometimes contradict themselves anyway. This philosophical failing can have small or great consequences for the cogency of the philosopher's views, but the presence of inconsistencies within a philosopher's viewpoint does not, by itself, disqualify the thinker from being a philosopher.

In any event, the consistency of Jesus' teachings cannot be so easily impugned. Jaspers cites just two cases of Jesus' supposed inconsistency and explores no possibilities for how these might be reconciled.[14] One example contrasts Jesus' teaching on not resisting evil (Matthew 5:38-42) with his statement that he came not to bring peace, but a sword. How can one be a sword-brandishing pacifist? Yet the passage about bringing a sword (Matthew 10:34-39) has nothing to do with self-defense or military situations, but with the fact that one's allegiance to Jesus will bring strife and division when one's family members do not follow Jesus. Therefore, the contradiction between Jesus' two statements is only apparent and not real.

Jaspers juxtaposes two more sayings of Jesus, which he claims are logically inconsistent. Jesus says that (1) those who are not against him are with him, but in another place he says that (2) those who are not with him are against him. Jaspers does not explain what the inconsistency between these statements might be, so we are left to guess. However, statement (2) could easily be seen as another way of putting statement (1). Thus there are those who are not against Jesus (that is, those who are with him) and there are those who are against Jesus (that is, those who are not with him). So, statements (1) and (2) seem correlative, not contradictory. The point in both cases is that there is no neutral ground; one must be either with him or against him.

But consider the events occasioning both of Jesus' statements. These two statements are made in different dialogical contexts and serve different purposes. The context for Jesus' statement that "those who are not against us are for us" is a case where those not in the inner circle of his disciples are seen casting out demons in Jesus' name (Mark 9:38-41). Jesus tells his disciples that these others are following him as well, although they are not known to the disciples. He explains, "No one who does a miracle in my name can in the next moment say anything bad about me." The context for the other statement, "he is who is not with me is against me, and he who does not gather with me scatters" (Matthew 12:30), is Jesus' confrontation with his theological opponents over his authority to drive out demons. Rather than widening the circle to include those who are already really following him (as in the first case), here Jesus is drawing a clear contrast between his followers and his detractors. While the contexts and purposes differ, there is no logical contradiction between Jesus' two statements.

Despite Jasper's claim that all Jesus' "direct statements are vehicles of a meaning which ultimately evades rational interpretation,"[15] Jaspers later approvingly quotes Hegel on Jesus: "Never have words so revolutionary been spoken, for everything otherwise looked on as valid is represented as indifferent, unworthy of consideration."[16] Whether this assessment of Jesus is accurate or not, it belies the notion that Jesus' message is "beyond rational interpretation," since Jaspers and Hegel *rationally* interpret Jesus' message as "revolutionary."

Jesus did not build a philosophical system in the same sense that Spinoza or Hegel did. Wittgenstein, arguably the most influential philosopher of the twentieth century, did not build a system at all, although he developed a distinctive philosophical method, which in some ways attempts to dissolve philosophical questions.[17] But the fact that Jesus did not "build" a philosophical system does not preclude the possibility that he thought in terms of a well-ordered and logically consistent account of reality and argued rationally with those who disputed it. If he thought and spoke in this manner, he was a philosopher indeed—and the most influential one in Western history.

Some may bar Jesus from the halls of philosophers by virtue of his prophetic or supernatural orientation toward teaching and the rest of his activities. It is assumed that a prophetic or oracular disposition makes philosophizing unnecessary or even counterproductive. If one receives a revelation from above, why argue from premise to conclusion? Why bother with induction, deduction, abduction, *reductio ad absurdum* or *a fortiori* arguments and the like when one is divinely inspired? Why criticize another's argument as fallacious? One would simply announce, declare, or proclaim—or bring down fire from heaven to end the argument entirely. Some Christians might even regard the notion that Jesus was a philosopher as ill-advised or blasphemous, since they take him to be God Incarnate. God has no need of human philosophy, after all.

These objections can be met in two ways. First, one need not bristle at the thought that even God Incarnate might philosophize with lesser beings, if it were for the purpose of engaging their God-given reasoning abilities. After all, the Apostle Paul—taken by many to be a superlative authority on Jesus—claimed that all knowledge and wisdom is found in Jesus Christ (Colossians 2:9). According to orthodox Christian thought, Jesus is not only divine, but truly human: "The Word became flesh" (John 1:14). However Christians may understand the relationship of deity and humanity in the person of Jesus, they must confess that God in Christ took on a genuinely human nature—reasoning abilities and all. As I will later argue, a close look at many passages in the Gospels reveals that Jesus does engage in careful reasoning regarding the afterlife, his own identity, political obligations, and more. He was not above a good debate. The Hebrew Scriptures, which Jesus revered, report that the prophet Isaiah, speaking as God's oracle, said, "'Come now, let us reason together,' says the Lord" (Isaiah 1:18). Jesus would agree.[18]

Second, and more generally, a claim to divine or supernatural inspiration (whether explicit or implicit) need not rule out reasoning and debate in principle. Authority can be established through sound reasoning and the ability to interact rationally with disputants. While the sacred books of theistic religions offer divine pronouncements *sans* argument, this is not the only mode of divine disclosure possible.

However, as we will discover later in this book, the tone, style, and content of Jesus' teachings and his debates with the leading thinkers of his day are very different from, say, the manner of Socrates, the quintessential philosopher (if unpublished). Jesus was a unique kind of philosopher. Jaspers underscores this in a passage worth examining:

> Jesus teaches by proclaiming the glad tidings, Socrates by compelling men to think. Jesus demands faith, Socrates an exchange of thought. Jesus speaks with direct earnestness, Socrates indirectly, even by irony. Jesus knows the kingdom of heaven and eternal life, Socrates has no definite knowledge of these matters and leaves the question open. But neither will let men rest. Jesus proclaims the only way; Socrates leaves man free, but keeps reminding him of his responsibility rooted in freedom. Both raise supreme claims. Jesus confers salvation. Socrates provokes men to look for it.[19]

I will argue that Jesus' "proclaiming glad tidings" (the gospel) is not incompatible with prodding people to think; he often did so. Demanding (or, better, encouraging or calling for) faith can occur alongside the rational exchange of ideas, and Jesus illustrated this. While Jesus spoke with "direct earnestness," sometimes he did communicate indirectly, especially in his parables. Jesus and Socrates do differ dramatically in that Jesus is never described as searching for truth or being gripped by uncertainty. Although Jesus proclaims ideas from a certainty of knowledge, he does leave some questions open (such as the number of those redeemed, why certain evils occur, and

9

the timing of his return). Socrates is a kind of philosophical goad and midwife while Jesus exhorts his listeners to be "born again"—but not without reason and argument in support of the faith and commitment enjoined.

---

[1] Jaroslav Pelikan, *Jesus through the Centuries: His Place in the History of Culture* (New York: Harper and Row, 1985), 1.

[2] On this movement, see Kelly James Clark, ed. *Philosophers Who Believe* (Downers Grove, IL: InterVarsity Press, 1993).

[3] Gordon Clark, *Thales to Dewey: A History of Philosophy* (Boston: Houghton Mifflin Company, 1957), 210.

[4] Dallas Willard, *The Divine Conspiracy* (San Francisco: HarperSanFrancisco, 1998), 134.

[5] Ibid., 95.

[6] Humphrey Carpenter, *Jesus* in *Founders of Faith*, (UK: Oxford University Press, 1986), 243.

[7] Ibid.

[8] Ibid., 244.

[9] Ibid., 241; emphasis in the original.

[10] Ibid., 243; emphasis added.

[11] Karl Jaspers, *The Great Philosophers*, Volume 1: *Socrates, Buddha, Confucius, Jesus*, ed. Hannah Arendt, trans. Ralph Manheim. (San Diego: Harcourt Brace Jovanovich, 1962), 71.

[12] Ibid., 75.

[13] Ibid., 94.

[14] Ibid., 71.

[15] Ibid., 71.

[16] Ibid. Jaspers does not cite his source for the quotation.

[17] See Jaako Hintikka, *On Wittgenstein* (Belmont, CA: Wadsworth-Thompson Learning, 2000).

[18] George Mavrodes explores different modes of divine revelation, which include revelation through reasoning, in *Revelation in Religious Belief* (Philadelphia: Temple University Press, 1988).

[19] Jaspers, 94.

2
Jesus in History

Even more so than with other philosophers, the historical details of Jesus' life are of paramount importance for accurately assessing his message and his identity. We know of nothing written by Jesus. The primary historical documents relating his life—the four Gospels of the New Testament—portray him through narratives that often involve discourses. Jesus' philosophy must be understood within the encounters and events narrated in the primary sources. His life setting and career cannot be separated from his argumentation and worldview. By contrast, the ideas of Aristotle, Descartes, Wittgenstein, or Weil may be discerned with minimal references to their biographies because they produced works meant to stand alone (although a knowledge of their historical background is very helpful for interpreting their works). Jesus' work was his life. His thought emerges from his encounters, sermons, debates, prayers, and actions.

Historicity and Philosophers

The historical details of Socrates' life are a bit murky, since he wrote nothing and our knowledge of him is dependent on Plato and a few other sources. This does not stop philosophers and students from assessing Socrates' contributions. Most people usually assume that Plato basically got it right. But if not, the character and philosophizing of Plato's Socrates are still compelling. Historians and philosophers have puzzled over Socrates, but there has never been "a quest for the historical Socrates" that matches the magnitude, duration, and intensity of "the quest for the historical Jesus."[1] And for good reason. Socrates founded no religion and no one worships him. But for over a span of

11

nearly two thousand years, millions have taken the New Testament Gospels as trustworthy accounts of the founder of their religion. Critics have questioned these convictions throughout history as well. One cannot settle this controversy in a chapter. However, in this chapter I will offer some background as to the historicity of these documents.

While many Christians regard the Gospels as divinely inspired and thus unerring documents, this perspective does not rule out a careful investigation of their nature and credentials. Divine inspiration need not mean anything like dictation from God to the writers. For example, the prologue to Luke's Gospel openly acknowledges that the author consulted various sources to present the history of Jesus:

> Many have undertaken to draw up an account of the things that have been fulfilled among us, just as they were handed down to us by those who from the first were eyewitnesses and servants of the word. Therefore, since I myself have carefully investigated everything from the beginning, it seemed good also to me to write an orderly account for you, most excellent Theophilus, so that you may know the certainty of the things you have been taught (Luke 1:1-4).

An interested person should admit that one's worldview will affect how one looks at the question of Jesus in history. Some have tried to eschew questions of historical scholarship entirely in favor of faith alone (fideism). Fideism removes all controls, or checks, on "faith," since it is untethered from historical or logical considerations. But as Ray Martin points out, this is a difficult stance when so much of popular and academic culture is taking up the question of "the historical Jesus." Conversely, some have just assumed that genuine historical investigation (about "the historical Jesus") can never agree with the tenets of Christianity (the "Christ of faith"). They thus prejudice the issue.[2] Some even claim that historians *qua* historians can never discuss the miraculous. A better approach makes use of historical evidence and arguments in assessing the documents.

The Textual Transmission of the Gospels

Documents from antiquity are sometimes condemned for being ancient. Something several thousand years old could not have been preserved with integrity. Too many omissions, additions, and distortions would have crept in. In addition, many worry that ancient records—especially the New Testament—have been translated from one language to another to another, so that their original meaning has been lost.

The question of a document's *integrity* (the preservation of the document's original form over time) is separate from its original *veracity* (the truth of what the document affirms). An original document filled with factual errors might have been transmitted without distortion. It could be a well-preserved fiction or even a fraud. But if there are no good reasons to trust an ancient document's integrity, its original veracity—or lack thereof—is of no consequence. Therefore, accurate transmission (integrity) is a necessary, but not sufficient, condition for trusting a document from antiquity.

The integrity of the Gospels—and the rest of the New Testament—holds up extraordinarily well, especially in relation to other ancient candidates. First, it is false that modern translations of the Gospels have been corrupted by being translated from language to language—say from Greek to Latin to German to English. Translators of modern English editions consult primarily ancient Greek manuscripts. Greek is the original language of the Gospels.

Second, well over five thousand partial or complete manuscripts of the Greek New Testament are available to scholars today.[3] The number and quality of these manuscripts have increased during the last few decades as archaeologists unearth more records of the world's most copied, recopied, and collected books. A fragment of the Gospel of John dates to the early second century, probably only a few decades after it was originally written. Given the large number and high quality of many of the early manuscripts, textual critics have a wealth of material from which to reconstruct the original records with a high degree of accuracy. No original manuscripts (autographs) are available for any ancient book, but historians often trust ancient records with far less textual attestation than that of the New Testament. For instance, Caesar's *The Gallic Wars* dates from 100-44 BC. The earliest copy is from AD 900, with a gap of 1,000 years. Only ten ancient copies of this document exist.[4]

A more germane comparison is found between the manuscripts of the canonical Gospels and various so-called Gnostic Gospels.[5] The discovery of the ancient Gnostic texts at Nag Hammadi in 1945 gave scholars access to a wealth of primary sources on ancient Gnosticism,[6] a multifaceted and somewhat mysterious religious movement that stressed the need to transcend matter through mystical illumination (or "gnosis"—Greek for knowledge). James Robinson, editor of *The Nag*

Hammadi Library, the authoritative collection of these documents, notes that many of the manuscripts are in very poor condition and, unlike the Bible, cannot be checked against a larger manuscript tradition outside of themselves.[7]

Modern translations of the New Testament Gospels make note of marginal or alternative readings, and of disputed sections (such as John 8:1-11 and Mark 16:9-20). The rest of these textually questionable sections of the Gospels make up no more than two or three verses and most only bring into question a small portion of one verse. These variations are noted in most modern translations. They do not bring into question any major event or teaching in Jesus' life.

External (Extra-Biblical) Sources on Jesus

Historical references to Jesus are not limited to the New Testament documents, although these are the most detailed accounts. Some have argued that the relative scarcity and thinness of extra-biblical references to Jesus imperils our knowledge of him, since we are thrown back to the Gospels. The Gospels are the oldest extant biographical documents about Jesus, although some of Paul's Epistles (which refer to Jesus, but are not biographies) were probably written earlier (in AD 50s). However, these facts do not jeopardize the trustworthiness of the Gospels. The records for any first century event are limited. Four biographies of Jesus and related references beyond them provide more than a sufficient amount of material, given the constraints of ancient history. Most written documents in ancient times focused on warfare, empires, and their leaders. If religious leaders were mentioned at all, it was because they occupied positions of institutional power. Jesus did not qualify for inclusion.

Several historically credible sources corroborate some Gospel claims about Jesus. The Jewish historian Josephus mentions Jesus twice in his *Antiquities* (AD 90-95), once in reference to James "the brother of Jesus who was called Christ,"[8] and once in a longer and disputed passage. Some think that later Christian editors added some favorable theological material.[9] But at a minimum it can be plausibly argued that Josephus writes that Jesus existed, was known as virtuous, was crucified, attracted many followers, worked wonders, and was believed to be risen from the dead.[10] Several decades after Josephus, the Roman historians Tacitus, Thallus, Pliny the Younger, and Suetonius also note the existence of Jesus, pertinent facts about his life, and the beliefs of his followers.[11]

Various relevant archaeological artifacts have been discovered, which date near or during the time of the events recorded in the Gospels. An ancient Jewish burial site unearthed in 1968 contains fifteen stone ossuaries holding the bones of thirty-five Jews who died in the fall of Jerusalem in AD 70. One victim is identified as Yohanan. Injuries to his bones indicate he was crucified. He was also buried in a private tomb, as was Jesus. This is significant because some scholars claim that victims of Roman crucifixion were not buried in this way, but left on the cross to be eaten by animals or tossed into group graves.[12] Other archaeological discoveries have also corroborated the existence of the pool of Bethesda, previously thought by some to be a literary invention of the Gospel of John (John 5:2);[13] the existence of Pontius Pilate, mentioned on a Latin plaque at Caesarea; the greatness of the temple in Jesus' day; the manner of tomb in which Jesus was buried; and many other items.[14]

The Gospels: What Kind of Documents?

The Gospels are not biographies in the modern sense because they lack material that would be included today, such as Jesus' physical appearance. They focus on the exceptional events accompanying his conception and birth, his public ministry of about three years, and especially the last week of his life before his betrayal and crucifixion. These documents are focused accounts of the significance of Jesus' life and teachings, not news reports or exhaustive biographies, neither of which existed in antiquity.

Some question the historical accuracy of the Gospels because their writers had a theological agenda. Luke's prologue explicitly states why he wrote his gospel (Luke 1:1-4). The Gospel of John offers a similar confession: "The man who saw it has given testimony, and his testimony is true. He knows that he tells the truth, and he testifies so that you also may believe" (John 19:35; see also 21:24). The Gospels of Matthew and Mark do not make overt statements to this effect, but were written by advocates of the early Jesus movement. Neutrality or detached objectivity—if possible at all—is not required for honest and accurate reporting. Nor was it known or idealized in antiquity. Historians take seriously the accounts of Jews, such as Elie Wiesel, who were tortured in concentration camps, despite the survivors' deeply committed perspectives.

The dimension of the miraculous is integral to all four Gospel accounts. The Gospels feature miraculous events, such as those

15

surrounding Jesus' birth, his ministry of healing the sick and raising the dead, his casting out of demons, his resurrection from the dead, and his ascension to heaven.

However, David Hume has argued against the rationality of believing any miracle-claim, basing this on the vast improbability of the "laws of nature" being "violated." He also impugns the credibility of the supposed witnesses to miracles and argues that the various miracle-claims offered by different religions cancel each other out.[15] All of Hume's in-principle arguments have been seriously challenged by professional philosophers and others.[16] Ray Martin has also pointed out that, although many contemporary scholars who study the Gospels claim to be "objective" and "disinterested" in their pursuits, they really presuppose a questionable "methodological naturalism," which absolutely precludes the supernatural from the purview of the historian.[17]

While the Gospels include miracles, other supernatural events, and theologically significant claims made by Jesus about himself, many scholars affirm that they read as historical, narrative, factual accounts—not as embellished and fantastic myths. Their credibility is supported by their references to specific people, places, and events surrounding the life of Jesus. John, considered the most theologically oriented of the Gospel writers, makes abundant references to particular buildings and landscapes, many of which have been corroborated from archeology.[18]

The historian Will Durant, no friend of religion, observes in his multi-volume series, *The Story of Civilization*, that the Gospel writers included many things that "mere inventors would have concealed," such as the apostles' prideful competition for high places in the kingdom of God, Peter's denial of Jesus, Jesus' ignorance of the future, and his despairing cry on the cross. Durant did not accept everything in the Gospels, but he did observe the basic marks of authenticity.[19] Biblical scholar A. E. Harvey concurs: "In general, one can say that the miracle stories in the Gospels are unlike anything else in ancient literature" because "they do not exaggerate the miracle or add sensational details." In other words, "they tell the story straight."[20]

The Authorship of the Four Gospels

Who wrote the Gospels and when? If they were written by eyewitnesses or those who interviewed eyewitnesses during a time shortly following the events they narrate, the Gospels gain credibility.

First, the outer limit for when the Gospels (and other New

Testament books) were written can be established by later Christian (postapostolic) sources that quote from them. Since historians are able to date these writings with some certainty, the Gospels must predate them. For example, Polycarp, who was a disciple of the Apostle John, quotes or refers to all four Gospels in a letter dated at about AD 110. Ignatius wrote seven short letters in about AD 108, which mention or quote from every Gospel. Clement, writing from Rome in about AD 96, mentions the Gospels of Matthew, Mark, and Luke by name.[21]

Second, many reputable scholars date the synoptic Gospels (Matthew, Mark, and Luke) at approximately AD 70 or earlier, with Mark usually dated first. John is usually dated sometime in the AD 90s, but some date him much earlier.[22] This places the accounts, whoever wrote them, just a few decades after the life of Jesus. Even the more liberal dating of Mark around AD 70 and Matthew and Luke sometime in the AD 80s still, by the standards of ancient historiography, puts the writings quite close to the events they record. Given the practice of memorizing the words of important teachers in an oral culture, this time gap is not damaging to the documents' historical reliability.[23]

To put this into comparative perspective, the Buddhist Scriptures were not written down for about five hundred years after the life of Buddha (BC 563-483). Buddhist scholar Edward Conze notes that while Christianity can distinguish its "initial tradition, embodied in the 'New Testament'" from a "continued tradition," consisting of reflections of the church fathers and councils, "Buddhists possess nothing that corresponds to the 'New Testament.' The 'continuing tradition' is all that is clearly attested."[24]

Third, the traditional authorship of the Gospels cannot be ruled out, although it is often questioned or rejected. The Gospels themselves were probably unsigned. The titles "The Gospel According to…" may have been added at a later date.[25] However, the earliest extra-biblical corroborating sources, which are from the second century, refer to the Gospels of Matthew and John as written by Jesus' disciples, Luke as written by a physician and companion of the Apostle Paul, and the Gospel of Mark as written by a companion of the Apostle Peter. There is also some internal evidence to support the traditional authors.[26]

If the traditional authorship holds, the Gospel material is based on eyewitness accounts of Jesus' life or on those who consulted eyewitnesses (Mark relying on the Apostle Peter) or at least inquired into the events at a time not far removed from them (Luke's investigations). Even if the traditional authorship is questioned or rejected, the documents are not rendered unreliable by that fact alone, given the considerations mentioned above.

The exact literary sources for the Gospels are much debated. The question of the sources for and relationship between Matthew, Mark, and Luke is known as "the synoptic problem." Many contemporary scholars believe that Mark was written first. Luke and Matthew rely on Mark's material quite often, but both also have material in common that is not in Mark. This material is conjectured to be from a lost document called *Q*, taken from the German word for source, *quelle*. Some reputable scholars still hold to the traditional view that Matthew was written first. The Gospel of John has a considerable amount of material in common with the synoptic Gospels; it also includes some elements that are unique. [27]

The differences in the Gospel accounts on matters of detail or chronology have been extensively studied, and differing conclusions have been reached. Nevertheless, rather than proving that some of the accounts are erroneous, these differences demonstrate an absence of a flat uniformity that would indicate collusion. Each Gospel writer wrote to a specific audience and shaped his account accordingly. Moreover, ancient writers were not always bound by strict chronology. They may organize historical accounts thematically rather than chronologically. A difference of perspective between several accounts does not necessarily imply a contradiction or a fabrication.

All the Gospels agree on the central facts of Jesus' life and death. The events surrounding his conception and birth were supernaturally tinged. His youth is not addressed in any detail. He was a carpenter by trade, as was his father. He began his public ministry at about age thirty after the endorsement of the prophet, John the Baptist. Jesus gathered disciples around himself, associated with various classes of people, including the despised of society (tax collectors, the handicapped, and women), preached the reality and pertinence of the kingdom of God, healed the sick, raised the dead, performed other types of miracles, and made dramatic theological claims about himself and his mission. He became progressively estranged from the religious establishment of the day and was put to death by crucifixion at the urging of that establishment and through the agency of the Roman state. He was buried and three days later rose from the dead and commissioned his followers to take his message to the ends of the earth until the end of the age. About all this, the Gospels are in straightforward agreement.

Jesus and Gnostic Documents

Some have hailed Gnostic documents as important sources about Jesus, despite their exclusion from the New Testament. The general Gnostic perspective asserts the worthlessness or evil of the physical world, affirms the existence of an ineffable highest realm called the *pleroma* (Greek for fullness), and rejects the God of the Old Testament as the Supreme Being. Gnosticism also advocates escape from the physical body through mystical self-knowledge and interprets the central human problem not as sin against God but as ignorance of one's true origin in the realm beyond matter. Some scholars, such as Elaine Pagels, have claimed that this mystical and dualistic tradition is on an equal or better footing than the Gospels with respect to the historical Jesus.[28] The Jesus Seminar includes "The Gospel of Thomas" in its main sources on Jesus. Hence the title of their book, *The Five Gospels*. Thomas is a collection of 114 short sayings by Jesus without a narrative context. Despite its title, modern scholars do not believe that Thomas, the disciple of Jesus, is its author. Less than half of these sayings roughly resemble material in the synoptic Gospels, but are shorn of the historical frameworks provided by Matthew, Mark, and Luke. The extra-canonical sayings emphasize the mystical and saving power of self-knowledge, an essential Gnostic theme not found in the four Gospels.

Of all the Gnostic accounts of Jesus, the Gospel of Thomas is the leading candidate to be dated possibly as early as the first century, although many date it sometime in the middle of the second century. The earliest references to The Gospel of Thomas in ancient literature come from Hippolytus and Origen in the third century. These very late references are unlike the plentiful references to the four Gospels, which date as far back as the early second century. Such a long silence would be unlikely if Thomas were indeed a first century document.[29] Furthermore, Thomas quotes sayings paralleled in every Gospel and in every putative Gospel source (Q, etc.). These facts strongly suggest that Thomas is dependent on these previous sources. For these and other reasons, many scholars contend that Thomas dates after the canonical Gospels, and that it is not an original source for material on Jesus but a reworking of earlier accounts.[30] All the other Gnostic texts date well into the second or third centuries and are clearly dependent on a preexistent Jesus tradition, which they reinterpret according to a worldview alien and antithetical to the Gospels.

Historian Philip Jenkins persuasively argues that much of the

19

contemporary interest in Gnostic "hidden gospels" (such as Thomas) is more a matter of ideological interest in overthrowing orthodoxy than of pure scholarship, since the evidence for the alternative sources is quite weak in relation to the canonical Gospels. Jenkins claims that the historical case for these alternative gospels is often stated in overly dramatic terms that obscure important issues.[31]

Nevertheless, some are attracted to the Gnostic materials because of their psychological insights, which differ considerably from perspectives in the canonical Gospels. Pagels find parallels between the Gnostic teachings and that of modern psychoanalysis, both of which emphasis inner knowledge as the source of human liberation.[32] Gnosticism claims that the inner or true self is divine, however, while most of psychoanalysis—especially the Freudian wing—works from a less metaphysically exalted sense of self. Psychiatrist and author Carl Jung (1875-1961), though not a biblical scholar, was significantly influenced by Gnosticism and claimed it was psychologically superior to orthodox Christianity.[33]

In light of the arguments of this chapter, the rest of this book will present the teachings and life of Jesus using the canonical Gospels as the main—but not only—sources of reference. This should offer further help to the reader in evaluating the internal evidence for the historicity and significance of the events described in these accounts.

---

[1] See Ben Witherington, III, *The Jesus Quest: The Third Search for the Jew of Nazareth* (Downers Grove, IL: InterVarsity Press, 1995).

[2] See Raymond Martin, *The Elusive Messiah: A Philosophical Overview of the Quest for the Historical Jesus* (Boulder, CO: Westview Press, 1999). For an argument for believing the New Testament without relying on historical evidence, see Alvin Plantinga, *Warranted Christian Belief* (New York: Oxford University Press, 2000).

[3] Kurt Aland and Barbara Aland, *The Text of the New Testament* (Grand Rapids, MI: Eerdmans, 1987), 87.

[4] F.F Bruce, *The New Testament Documents: Are They Reliable?* rev. ed. (Downers Grove, IL: InterVarsity Press, 1960), 16.

[5] The title "Gospel" is not fitting, since the literary genre is not that of the canonical Gospels, although the Gnostic texts do claim to give accounts of Jesus' life and teachings.

[6] Much was known previously of the basic Gnostic worldview through the writings of the church fathers and a few scattered other sources.

[7] James Robinson, ed. *The Nag Hammadi Library* (San Francisco: Harper and Row, 1988), 2.

[8] Josephus, *Antiquities* 20:9.

[9] Ibid., 18:3.

[10] See Robert E. Van Voorst, *Jesus Outside the New Testament: An Introduction to Ancient Evidence* (Grand Rapids, MI: Eerdmans, 2000), 81-104.

[11] Ibid., 19-53.

[12] Jeffrey Sheler, *Is The Bible True?* (Grand Rapids, MI: Zondervan Publishers, 1999), 110-111.

[13] R.T. France, *The Evidence for Jesus* (Downers Grove, IL: InterVarsity Press, 1986), 131-132

[14] Ibid., 140-157.

[15] See David Hume, *Enquiry Concerning Human Understanding*, "Of Miracles," many editions.

[16] See C.S. Lewis, *Miracles: A Preliminary Study* (New York: Simon and Schuster, 1975; orig. pub. 1947); R. Douglas Geivett, Gary R. Habermas, *In Defense of Miracles: A Comprehensive Case for God's Action in History* (Downers Grove, IL: InterVarsity Press, 1997); and J. A. Cover, "Miracles and Christian Theism," in *Reason for the Hope Within*, ed. Michael M. Murray (Grand Rapids, MI: Eerdmans, 1998), 345-374.

[17] Martin, 99-120.

[18] Paul Barnett, *Is the New Testament History?* (Ann Arbor, MI: Servant Publications, 1986), 64.

[19] Will Durant, *Caesar and Christ*, vol. 2, *The Story of Civilization* (New York: Simon and Schuster, 1944), 557.

[20] A. E. Harvey, *Jesus and the Constraints of History* (Philadelphia: Westminster, 1982), 41-42.

[21] Barnett, 38-39.

[22] John A.T. Robinson dates all the Gospels before AD 70, largely because none of them mention the fall of Jerusalem in AD 70. See *Redating the New Testament* (Philadelphia: Westminster Press, 1976).

[23] Craig Blomberg, *The Historical Reliability of the Gospels* (Downers Grove, IL: InterVarsity Press, 1987), 26-27.

[24] "Introduction," in *Buddhist Scriptures*, ed. Edward Conze (New York: Penguin Books, 1959), 11-12.

[25] Martin Hengel disputes the traditional notion of unsigned Gospels in *The Four Gospels and the One Gospel of Jesus Christ* (Trinity Press International, 2000).

[26] See the sections relating to authorship in Douglas Moo, D. A. Carson, and Leon Morris, *An Introduction to the New Testament* (Grand Rapids, MI: Zondervan Publishing Company, 1992).

[27] See Craig Blomberg, *The Historical Reliability of John's Gospel:*

Issues and Commentary (Leicester and Downers Grove: InterVarsity Press, 2002), and Millard Erickson, *The Word Became Flesh: An Incarnational Theology* (Grand Rapids, MI: Baker Books, 1992), 409-430.

[28] Elaine Pagels, *The Gnostic Gospels* (New York: Random House, 1979).

[29] Gregory A. Boyd, *Cynic Sage or Son of God?* (Wheaton, IL: Victor Books, 1995), 134.

[30] Blomberg, *Historical Reliability of The Gospels*, 211-212.

[31] See Phillip Jenkins, *The Hidden Gospels* (New York: Oxford University Press, 2001).

[32] Pagels, 119-141.

[33] C. J. Jung, *Memories, Dreams, and Reflections* (New York: Vintage Books, 1973), 192.

3

Jesus' Use of Argument

In evaluating the identity and teachings of Jesus, we need to consider not only the historical attestation of the Gospels, but also the internal evidence of Jesus' life and teaching as given by the Gospel writers. Do these historical documents have the "ring of truth"? One must judge for oneself. This and the following chapters will focus on Jesus' teachings, his ways of arguing about his worldview and his own identity. We begin by considering whether or not Jesus engaged in significant logical arguments worthy of a philosopher. Many stress that Jesus was more than a philosopher. Nevertheless, the Gospel accounts that describe the supernatural Jesus also contain argumentative encounters that reveal a strong concern for logic and argument.

Did Jesus Disparage Rationality?

Biblical scholar John Stott observes that Jesus was a "controversialist" in that he was not "broad-minded." Jesus did not countenance every and any view on important subjects, but instead engaged in extensive disputes, some quite heated, mostly with the Jewish intellectual leaders of his day. He was not afraid to cut against the grain of popular opinion if he deemed it to be wrong. He spoke often and passionately about the value of truth and the dangers of error, and he gave arguments to support truth and oppose error.[1]

Jesus' use of logic had a particular tenor to it, notes philosopher Dallas Willard.

Jesus' aim in utilizing logic is not to win battles, but to achieve understanding or insight in his hearers. . . . That is, he does not

23

try to make everything so explicit that the conclusion is forced down the throat of the hearer. Rather, he presents matters in such a way that those who wish to know can find their way to, can come to, the appropriate conclusion as something they have discovered—whether or not it is something they particularly care for.[2]

Willard also argues that a concern for logic requires not only certain intellectual skills but also certain character commitments regarding the importance of logic and the value of truth in one's life. A thoughtful person must choose to esteem logic and argument through focused concentration, reasoned dialogue, and a willingness to follow the truth wherever it may lead. This cognitive orientation places demands on the moral life. Besides resolution, tenacity, and courage, one must shun hypocrisy (defending oneself against facts and logic for ulterior motives) and superficiality (adopting opinions with a glib disregard for their logical support). Willard takes Jesus to be a model in this, as does James Sire.[3]

Nevertheless, philosopher Michael Martin alleges that the Jesus of the Gospel accounts (the reliability of which he questions) "does not exemplify important intellectual virtues. Both his words and his actions seem to indicate that he does not value reason and learning." Jesus based "his entire ministry on faith."[4] He interprets Jesus' statement about the need to become like children to enter the kingdom of heaven (Matthew 18:3) as praising uncritical belief. Martin charges that when Jesus did give any reason to accept his teaching, it was either that the kingdom was at hand or that those who believed would go to heaven but those who disbelieved would go to hell. Supposedly, "no rational justification was ever given for these claims."[5] For Jesus, unreasoning faith was good; rational demonstration and criticism were wrong.

These are damning charges against the claim that Jesus was a philosopher who valued reasoning and who held a well-developed worldview. I believe that Martin has misconstrued Jesus' statement about becoming like a child. If the rest of the Gospel material consistently showed Jesus avoiding or condemning any rational assessment of his teachings or claims, Martin's contention would be vindicated. As we shall see, this is not the case. The same Jesus who valued children also said, "Love the Lord your God with all your heart and with all your soul and with all your *mind*" (Matthew 22:37; emphasis added).

Jesus very likely praised children for the same reasons that people customarily praise them. Children are not viewed as models because they are irrational or immature, but because they are innocent and wholehearted in their love, devotion, and enthusiasm for life. Children are also esteemed because they can be very humble, having not learned the pretensions and posturings of the adult world of ego and manipulation. The story in Matthew 18 has just this favorable view of children in mind. Jesus is asked by his disciples, "Who is the greatest in the kingdom of heaven?" After calling a child and having him stand among them, Jesus replies:

> I tell you the truth, unless you change and become like little children, you will never enter the kingdom of heaven. Therefore, those who humble themselves like this child are the greatest in the kingdom of heaven. And whoever welcomes a little child like this in my name welcomes me (Matthew 18:3-5).

The meaning of "become like little children" is not "become uncritical and unthinking" (*pace* Martin), but "become humble." Jesus spoke much of humility (as do the Hebrew Scriptures), and never associated humility with stupidity, ignorance, or gullibility.[6] Jesus did thank God for revealing the Gospel to the humble and not to the supposedly wise and understanding. This, however, does not imply that intelligence was a detriment to believing Jesus' message, but that some of the intellectual/religious leaders of the day could not grasp it, largely because of its humbling consequences (see Matthew 11:25-26).

Unless humility is incompatible with intelligence and rational investigation, there is no reason to believe that Jesus prizes gullibility or credulity. Most of us have met a few valued women and men who have been both tough-minded and softhearted. They pursue truth reasonably, but not arrogantly or pridefully. Moreover, children often ask searching and difficult questions—even of a philosophical nature. It seems that Martin imposes an unfair meaning on Jesus' words.

Martin also alleges that the only reasons Jesus gives in support of his teaching are that the kingdom of God is at hand, and that those who fail to believe will fail to receive the heavenly benefits accorded to those with faith.[7] Is this true?

First, Jesus spoke much of the kingdom of God, and used it as a justification for some of his teaching and preaching. The first message of his public career was: "Repent, for the kingdom of heaven is near" (Matthew 4:17). Jesus was admonishing people to reorient their lives spiritually and morally because God was breaking into history in an unparalleled and dramatic fashion. This is not necessarily an irrational or unfounded claim if (a) God was acting in this manner in Jesus' day and (b) one can find evidence for the emergence of the kingdom, chiefly through the actions of Jesus himself. The Gospels present the kingdom as uniquely present in the teaching and actions of Jesus. So, Jesus claims that "if I drive out demons by the Spirit of God, then the kingdom of God has come upon you" (Matthew 12:28). Since his audience took him to be driving out demons with singular authority, Jesus was giving a *modus ponens* argument. If P, then Q; P, therefore Q. This brief observation does not settle all the logical or evidential questions raised, but it does indicate that Jesus' argument for the kingdom of God can serve as a logical support for his teaching and purpose. He is not merely making assertions or ungrounded threats, and expecting compliance in a childish or cowardly way.

Second, Jesus' use of the concept of God's judgment or reward did not supercede or replace his use of arguments. His normal argument form was not the following: "If you believe X, you will be rewarded. If you don't believe X, you will lose that reward. Therefore, believe X." When Jesus issued warnings and made promises relating one's conduct in this life to the afterlife (see John 3:16-18), he spoke more as a prophet than a philosopher. Addressing those who would be persecuted and falsely charged because of their allegiance to him, Jesus said, "Rejoice and be glad, because great is your reward in heaven" (Matthew 5:12). Whether Jesus' words in this matter are trustworthy depends on his moral and spiritual authority, not on his specific arguments at every point. If we have reason to deem him authoritative, we may rationally believe these pronouncements, just as we believe various other authorities whom we deem trustworthy on the basis of their credentials and track record.

Escaping the Horns of a Dilemma

We need to consult the record to find whether or not Jesus prized a well-developed rationality. Several examples illustrate Jesus' ability to escape deftly from between the horns of a dilemma when challenged. Two telling cases come from Matthew, chapter 22.

Disciples of the Pharisees and several Herodians asked Jesus a controversial political question. The Pharisees, powerful religious leaders of the Jews, were ardent nationalists who opposed the rule that Rome had imposed on the Jews in Palestine. The Herodians, on the other hand, were followers and defenders of the Herods, the Roman rulers who strictly governed Palestine. After some initial flattery about Jesus' integrity, they tried to spring a trap. "Tell us then, what is your opinion? Is it right to pay taxes to Caesar or not?" (Matthew 22:17).

Jesus faced a tough dilemma. If he sided with the Pharisees, he might be seen as an insurrectionist and a dangerous element (as were the Zealots, Jews who defended violent revolution against the state). If Jesus affirmed paying taxes, he would be viewed as selling out to a secular and ungodly power instead of honoring Israel's God. He would be denounced as disloyal. This was not a "win-win" situation. As Matthew tells us, the Pharisees had "laid plans to trap him in his words" (Matthew 22:15).

Jesus responded by asking for the coin used to pay the tax, a denarius. He asked, "Whose portrait is this? And whose inscription?" They replied that it was Caesar's. Jesus uttered the now famous words, "Give to Caesar what is Caesar's and to God what is God's." At this the delegation dispersed in amazement at his answer (Matthew 22:18-22).

Jesus displays a cool head and sharp mind. When confronted with a classic dilemma pertaining to what we would call church/state relations, he finds a way logically to escape from between the horns of the dilemma. Jesus gives a place to the rule of Caesar under God without making Caesar God. Caesar's portrait on the coin (a bust of Tiberius) had an inscription ascribing deity to the emperor. When he differentiates Caesar from God, he strips Caesar of his supposed deity.

Jesus' saying, while short and pithy, has inspired many political philosophers to explicate and apply the concept of a limited state in relation to religion and the rest of culture. While not offering a developed political philosophy (no one was asking for that, anyway), Jesus shows a deep awareness of the issues involved and responds intelligently under public pressure. On other occasions, as well, Jesus shows himself to be neither a disloyal Jew, nor an insurrectionist. He refers to God, not Caesar, as the "Lord of heaven and earth" (Matthew 11:25), but does not eliminate temporal authority. At his trial preceding his execution, Jesus informs Pilate, "You would have no power over me if it were not given to you from above" (John 19:11).

Immediately after the question about taxation, Matthew records another intellectual encounter. The Sadducees, another influential Jewish group, try to corner Jesus on a question about the afterlife. They, unlike the Pharisees, did not believe in life after death, nor in angels or spirits (although they were theists), and they granted special authority only to the Pentateuch (the first five books of the Hebrew Bible). They remind Jesus of Moses' command "that if a man dies without having children, his brother must marry the widow and have children for him." (This is called levirate marriage.) Then they propose a thought experiment in which the same woman is progressively married to and widowed by seven brothers, none of which sire any children by her. Then the woman dies. "Now then, at the resurrection, whose wife will she be of the seven, since all of them were married to her?" they ask pointedly (Matthew 22:23-28).

The argument is clever. The Sadducees know that Jesus reveres the law of Moses, as they do. They also know that Jesus, unlike themselves, teaches that there will be a resurrection of the dead. They think that these two beliefs are logically inconsistent; they cannot both be true. The woman cannot be married to all seven at the resurrection (Mosaic law did not allow polyandry), nor is there any reason why she should be married to any one out of the seven (thus honoring monogamy). Therefore, they figure, Jesus must either come against Moses or deny the afterlife if he is to remain free from contradiction. They are presenting this as a logical dilemma: either A (Moses' authority) or B (the afterlife), not neither A or B, and not both A and B.

As we noted, Karl Jaspers and Humphrey Carpenter claim that Jesus was not concerned about consistency, and Michael Martin asserts that Jesus praised uncritical faith over reason and induced belief only through rewards and punishments. If these charges were correct, one might expect Jesus (a) to dodge the question with a pious and unrelated utterance or (b) to threaten hell for those who dare question his authority or (c) simply assert two logically incompatible propositions with no hesitation or shame. Instead, Jesus forthrightly says that the Sadducees are in error because they have failed to know the Scripture or the power of God.

> At the resurrection people will neither marry nor be given in marriage; they will be like the angels in heaven. But about the resurrection of the dead—have you not read what God said to you, "I am the God of Abraham, the God of Isaac, and the God of Jacob"? He is not the God of the dead but of the living (Matthew 22:30-32).

Jesus' response has an astuteness that may not be obvious. First, he challenged their assumption that belief in the resurrection means that one is committed to believing that all of our pre-mortem institutions will be retained in the postmortem, resurrected world. None of the Hebrew Scriptures teaches this, and Jesus did not believe it. Thus, the dilemma dissolves. It is a false dilemma because Jesus states a *tertium quid*: there is no married state at the resurrection. Second, as part of his response to their logical trap, Jesus compares the resurrection state of men and women to that of the angels, thus challenging the Sadducees' disbelief in angels. (Although the Sadducees did not believe in angels, they knew that their fellow Jews who did believe in angels thought that angels did not marry or procreate.) Third, Jesus cites a text from the Sadducees' own esteemed Scriptures (Exodus 3:6), where God declares to Moses from the burning bush that he is the God of Abraham, Isaac, and Jacob. Jesus could have cited a variety of texts from writings outside the Pentateuch in support of the resurrection, such as the prophets (Daniel 12:2) or Job (19:25-27), but instead he deftly argues from their own trusted sources, which he also endorsed. Fourth, Jesus capitalizes on the verb tense of the verse he quotes. God is (present tense) the God of Abraham, Isaac, and Jacob, all of whom who had already died at the time God uttered this to Moses. He did not cease to be their God at their earthly demise. God did not say, "I was their God" (past tense). God is the God of the living, which includes even the "dead" patriarchs. Matthew adds that "when the crowds heard this, they were astonished at his teaching," for Jesus had "silenced the Sadducees" (Matthew 22:33-34).

A Fortiori Arguments

Jesus was fond of *a fortiori* (Latin: "from the stronger") arguments, which often appear in pithy but persuasive forms in the Gospels.[8] These arguments have this logical structure:

1. The truth of A is accepted.
2. The support for the truth of B (which is relevantly similar to A) is even stronger than that of A.
3. Therefore, if the truth of A must be accepted, then so must the truth of B.

An *a fortiori* argument can misfire in three ways. First, the acceptance of A as true may be wrong. If so, the conclusion will not follow. For example, "If an amateur astrologer makes successful predictions, how much more accurate will a professional astrologer be." Second, the relationship between A and B may not be *a fortiori*. For example, in Plato's *Crito*, he argues that if we owe respect and gratitude to our parents and should do them no harm, we owe even greater respect and gratitude to the laws of Athens and should do

29

nothing to oppose them. One might argue that the loyalty owed to parents is greater than or equal to that of the state. If so, then there is no *a fortiori* relationship. Third, B may not be relevantly similar to A, thus breaking the analogy. For example, "If shouting is acceptable at a baseball game, how much more so is it acceptable at a college graduation." Since baseball games and graduations are quite dissimilar public environments with different norms of propriety, the connection breaks down and the attempted *a fortiori* argument founders.

Consider Jesus' argument against the Pharisees concerning the propriety of his performing a healing on the Sabbath:

> I did one miracle [on the Sabbath], and you are all astonished. Yet, because Moses gave you circumcision (although actually it did not come from Moses, but from the patriarchs), you circumcise a child on the Sabbath. Now if a child can be circumcised on the Sabbath so that the law of Moses may not be broken, why are you angry with me for healing the whole person on the Sabbath? Stop judging by mere appearances, and make a right judgment (John 7:21-24).

Jesus' argument can be formalized this way:

1. The Pharisees endorse circumcision even when done on the Sabbath, the day of rest from work. (Circumcision was performed eight days after the birth of a male, which sometimes fell on the seventh day of the week, the Sabbath.) This does not violate the Sabbath laws because it is an act of goodness.
2. Healing the whole person is even more important and beneficial than circumcision, which only affects one aspect of the male.
3. Therefore, if circumcision on the Sabbath is not a violation of the Sabbath, neither is Jesus' healing of a person on the Sabbath.

Jesus' concluding comment, "Stop judging by appearances, and make a right judgment," is a rebuke to their illogic, their inconsistency in applying their own moral and religious principles.

Jesus argues in a similar form in several passages regarding the meaning of the Sabbath. After healing a crippled woman on the Sabbath, the synagogue ruler was indignant, and said: "There are six days for work. So come and be healed on those days, not on the Sabbath!" Jesus reminds him that one may lawfully untie one's ox or donkey on the Sabbath and lead it to water. "Then should not this woman, a daughter of Abraham, whom Satan has kept bound for eighteen long years, be set free on the Sabbath day from what bound her?" Jesus' argument is thus:

1. The Jews lawfully release animals from their confinement on the Sabbath out of concern for the animal's well-being.
2. A woman's well-being (being freed from a chronic, debilitating illness) is far more important than watering an animal.
3. Therefore, if watering an animal on the Sabbath is not a Sabbath violation, then Jesus' healing the woman on the Sabbath is not a violation of the Sabbath.

Luke records that when Jesus "said this, all his opponents were humiliated, but the people were delighted with all the wonderful things he was doing" (Luke 13:10-17).

Jesus' Appeal to Evidence in Argument

Despite the frequent portrayal of Jesus as a mystical figure who called people to adopt an uncritical faith, he frequently appealed to evidence to confirm his claims. John the Baptist, who was languishing in prison, sent messengers to ask Jesus the question: "Are you the one who was to come, or should we expect someone else?" (Matthew 11:3). This may seem an odd question from a man the Gospels present as the prophetic forerunner of Jesus, who had proclaimed Jesus to be the Messiah. However, Jesus does not rebuke the question by saying, "You must have faith; suppress your doubts." Nor does he scold, "If you don't believe, you'll go to hell and miss heaven." Instead, Jesus rehearses the distinctives of his ministry.

Go back and report to John what you hear and see: The blind receive sight, the lame walk, those who have leprosy are cured, the deaf hear, the dead are raised, and the good news is preached to the poor. Blessed is the one who does not fall away on account of me (Matthew 11:4-6; see also Luke 7:22).

31

Jesus' works of healing and teaching are meant to serve as positive evidence of his messianic identity, because they fulfill the messianic predictions of the Hebrew Scriptures.[9] What Jesus is claiming, put into an explicit argument form, is this:

1. If one does X-kinds of actions (the acts cited above), then one is the Messiah.
2. I am doing X-kinds of actions.
3. Therefore, I am the Messiah.

This is a *modus ponens* form of argument (If P, then Q; P, therefore, Q), which invokes empirical claims—Jesus' works—as its factual basis. The acts he cites are meant to point out necessary and sufficient criteria for identifying the Messiah, "the one who was to come."

After another healing on the Sabbath, Jesus is challenged by the religious leaders for breaking the sacred day by working. He responds, "My Father is always at his work to this very day, and I, too, am working." Jesus' disputants view this as blasphemy, because "not only was he breaking the Sabbath, but he was even calling God his own Father, making himself equal with God" (John 5:17-18). Ancient Jews sometimes referred to God as Father, but not with the possessive, "my Father," since they thought this established too close a relationship between the Creator and the creature.

Instead of disavowing this conclusion, Jesus makes six other statements that reinforce their conclusion that he is, in fact, "making himself equal with God."

1. He acts in the same manner as the Father by giving life to the dead (5:19-21).
2. He judges as a representative, and with the authority, of the Father (5:22, 27).
3. If he is not honored, God the Father is not honored (5:23).
4. The one who believes in Jesus believes also in God (5:24-25)
5. Like God (see Deuteronomy 30:20), he has life in himself (5:26).
6. He is in complete agreement with the Father, whom he perfectly pleases—a claim no Jew in the Hebrew Scriptures ever made (5:30).

These further claims provide more reasons (if true) for thinking that Jesus is "equal with God." However, he does not leave it at the level of

32

assertion. He appeals to evidence to which his hearers would have had access:

1. John the Baptist, a respected prophet, has testified as to Jesus' identity (5:31-35).
2. Jesus' miraculous works also testify to his identity (5:36).
3. The Father testifies to Jesus' identity (5:37).
4. The Scriptures likewise testify to his identity (5:39).
5. Moses testifies to who Jesus is (5:46).

Although we cannot take the time to discuss the strength of these arguments, the upshot is that Jesus reasoned with his intellectual opponents.[10] He did not simply declare propositions, threaten punishments to those who disagreed, or attack his adversaries as unspiritual. He highly valued argument and evidence.

Reductio Ad Absurdum Arguments

A *reductio ad absurdum* argument form is commonly used (and abused) by philosophers and others. When successful it is a powerful refutation of an illogical position. The term means "reduction to absurdity." The argument takes one or more claims and demonstrates that they lead to an absurd or contradictory conclusion. This proves that the original ideas must be false. For such an argument to work logically, the entailment relationship between the terms must hold and the supposed absurdity must truly be absurd. Consider one failed attempt at *reductio ad absurdum*:

1. If the southern American slaves are freed, then women will want the vote and get it.
2. The idea of women getting the vote is absurd.
3. Therefore, the southern slaves should not be freed.

This pathetic argument (which was made by some slave holders before the Civil War) fails because the idea of adult women exercising the franchise is not absurd. But consider Jesus' use of *reductio ad absurdum*.

Jesus asked the Pharisees, "What do you think about the Christ? Whose son is he?" The reply was, "The son of David." Jesus responded, "How is it then that David, speaking by the Spirit, calls him

'Lord'? For he says, 'The Lord said to my Lord: Sit at my right hand until I put your enemies under your feet.'" By quoting Psalm 110:1, Jesus appealed to a source that the Pharisees accepted. He concluded matters with the question, "If then David calls him 'Lord,' how can he be his son?" which Matthew records as silencing the audience (Matthew 22:41-46). The argument can be stated as follows:

1. If the Christ is merely the human descendent of David, David could not have called him "Lord."
2. David did call the Christ "Lord" in Psalm 110:1.
3. To believe Christ was David's Lord and merely his human descendent (who could not be his Lord) is absurd.
4. Therefore, Christ is not merely the human descendent of David.

Jesus' point was not to deny the Christ's ancestral lineage to David, since Jesus himself is called "the Son of David" in the Gospels (Matthew 1:1), and since Jesus accepts the title without rebuke (Matthew 20:30-31). Rather, Jesus is denying that the Christ is *merely* the son of David; he is also Lord, and was so at the time of David. By using this *reductio ad absurdum* argument, Jesus attempts to expand his audience's understanding of who the Christ is and that he himself is the Christ.[11]

Jesus employs another *reductio ad absurdum* when the Pharisees attempt to discredit his reputation as an exorcist by charging him with driving out demons by the agency of Beelzebub, the prince of demons. In other words, his reputation as a holy wonderworker is undeserved. What seem to be godly miracles really issue from a demonic being. In response, Jesus takes their premise and derives an absurdity:

> Every kingdom divided against itself will be ruined, and every city or household divided against itself will not stand. If Satan drives out Satan, he is divided against himself. How then can his kingdom stand? And if I drive out demons by Beelzebub, by whom do your people drive them out? (Matthew 12:25-27).

Put formally:

1. If Satan were divided against himself, his kingdom would be ruined.
2. But it is not ruined (since demonic activity continues). To

34

think otherwise is absurd.

3. Therefore (a), Satan does not drive out Satan.
4. Therefore (b), Jesus cannot free people from Satan by satanic power.

Moreover, since the Pharisees also practiced exorcism, if Jesus casts out demons by Satan, then the Pharisees must grant that they too drive out demons by Satan (Matthew 12:27). But they themselves must reject this accusation as absurd. Therefore, Jesus cannot be accused of exercising satanic power through his exorcisms. He marshals two powerful *reductio* arguments in just a few sentences.

This summary does not do justice to the wealth of Jesus' arguments. We will discover some of Jesus' other arguments in the following chapters. However, our sampling of Jesus' reasoning—using the *tertium quid, a fortiori, modus ponens*, appeals to evidence, and *reductio ad absurdum*—bring into serious question the indictment that Jesus praised uncritical faith over reasoning and that he had no truck with logical consistency. Our next three chapters explore Jesus' worldview, which itself is subject to rational debate and detailed analysis.

---

[1] John R. K. Stott, *Christ the Controversialist* (Downers Grove, IL: InterVarsity Press, 1970), 18.

[2] Dallas Willard, "Jesus, the Logician," *Christian Scholars Review* XXVIII, no. 4 (1999): 607.

[3] James Sire, *Habits of the Mind: Intellectual Life as a Christian Calling* (Downers Grove, IL: InterVarsity Press, 2000), 203.

[4] Michael Martin, *The Case Against Christianity* (Philadelphia: Temple University Press, 1991), 167.

[5] Ibid.

[6] See Matthew 23:1-12; Luke 14:1-14; 18:9-14.

[7] Martin, 167.

[8] See, for example, Luke 11:11-2; 12:4-5; 12:6-7; 12:24; 12:27-28; 12:54-56; 13:14-16; 14:1-5; 18:1-8.

[9] See Isaiah 26:19; 29:18-19; 35:4-6; 61:1-2.

[10] I am indebted here to James W. Sire's treatment. See his *Habits of the Mind*, 191-192.

[11] See also Acts 2:29-34; 13:39; Hebrews 1:5-13.

4
Jesus' Metaphysics

Jesus' Metaphysics

Jesus did not construct a metaphysical system in the manner of Aristotle, Plato, or Kant. Few philosophers have. However, Jesus did communicate with strong conviction about his own identity and purpose, the reality of the Creator and Lawgiver, the spiritual realm, the nature of human persons, history, and the afterlife. If metaphysics is defined as the philosophy of being in all its dimensions, Jesus possessed a developed metaphysics. In this he was quite unlike some contemporary philosophers, who disparage such grand perspectives or metanarratives as outmoded, ill-conceived, or intrinsically oppressive.

Unlike the Buddha and Confucius, Jesus articulated clear ideas about the reality of God, and he made that reality the core of his teaching. As a religious Jew, he believed in the God of creation and covenant. God, human liberation, and the history of Israel and the entire cosmos were closely related. Jesus, as opposed to Buddha, did not articulate a method of liberation that was agnostic or neutral with respect to great metaphysical questions. Although later Buddhist writings can be metaphysically sophisticated, and the Buddha was not entirely without a metaphysic, he considered questions about creation and divine reality to be unedifying. "The Blessed One" would not speak to "whether the world is eternal or temporal, finite or infinite; whether the life principle is identical with the body, or something different; whether the Perfect One continues after death."[1]

Jesus, conversely, believed that substantial metaphysical knowledge was possible, desirable, and valuable—indeed vital—for spiritual liberation. Nevertheless, Jesus declined to answer some philosophical questions that he took to be unrelated or detrimental to spiritual advancement (see Luke 13:22-24).

Jesus: Theist

Jesus' public ministry commenced with his proclamation of the kingdom of God and its implications for life (Matthew 4:17). The key point of Jesus' teaching on the kingdom is that God exists and is decisively involved in both human and cosmic affairs. All of Jesus' teachings are organically related to his understanding of God. Without the concept of God, Jesus' teachings unravel. According to him, one's knowledge of God is pivotal for one's spiritual state, character, and destiny. During a theological dispute about the afterlife, Jesus rebuked some religious leaders by saying, "You are in error because you do not know the Scriptures or the power of God" (Matthew 22:29).

Jesus advocated a theistic worldview: There is one God who is (1) personal, (2) knowable, (3) worthy of adoration, worship, and service, (4) separate from the creation ontologically, but (5) involved with creation through providence, prophecy, and miracle.[2] But Jesus did not argue for the existence of God philosophically—in the sense of giving theistic proofs—nor did he engage in speculation about God's character or call for a blind leap of faith in the dark in order to believe in God. Instead, he spoke of God with conviction and certainty. In Jesus' milieu, unlike our own, there were few atheists, skeptics, relativists, or agnostics. In the Gospels, Jesus is never questioned about the existence of God. The main controversies for Jews pertained to the nature of true religion as revealed in the Hebrew Scriptures, and how to understand God's dealings with his chosen people.

Like most of his Jewish contemporaries, Jesus believed in the existence of God as an active Spirit (John 4:24), who was evidenced by all of creation, who had made a covenant with the Jews, delivered his people from Egypt, sent the prophets, and acted decisively throughout history, as recorded in the Hebrew Scriptures. From his comment that "the Scripture cannot be broken" (John 10:35) and his statement that he has not come to abolish the Law or the Prophets but to fulfill them (Matthew 5:17), it is clear that Jesus upheld the truth of the Scriptures, and so maintained the Jewish view of God.

Jesus often impressed upon his audience the unique relationship between himself and the God of the Jews. After being asked about the way to the Father, Jesus affirmed that, "Anyone who has seen me has seen the Father" (John 14:9). He also claimed to drive out demons "by the Spirit of God," indicating the presence of God's kingdom in his own person (Matthew 12:28).

Jesus believed in a personal God who was transcendent in being, immanent, and personal. Some, however, have claimed that Jesus was a guru, yogi, or swami, whose teachings can be interpreted in a pantheistic manner. Jesus, some submit, acknowledged a God who was an impersonal force, principle, or consciousness, a divine reality of which humans were innately a part This notion has become quite popular in the last few decades and has been defended in a number of books by Joseph Campbell and Deepak Chopra. If it appeals to the Gospels at all, this theory is usually based on a few questionable interpretations of Jesus' statements. I will address one such claim.

In a dispute with religious leaders about Jesus' identity, he is asked to reveal plainly whether or not he is the Christ (Messiah). Jesus claims that he has already told them, that his miracles speak for him, that he gives eternal life to his followers, and that he and the Father are one. His opponents argue that he blasphemes by claiming to be God. Jesus replies by quoting a text from the Hebrew Bible where God said, "You are 'gods.'" He then argues *a fortiori* that if God called them gods, "to whom the word of God came—and the Scripture cannot be broken—what about the one whom the Father set apart as his very own and sent into the world?" (John 10:22-36).

The text to which Jesus referred (Psalm 82:6) was addressed to political leaders who were called "gods" because of their divinely delegated authority. They were not God, the ultimate reality, since the psalm goes on to say that they will perish like ordinary mortals. Therefore, far from claiming that all people are divine, Jesus is arguing that if mere humans can be called "gods," how much more can Jesus himself be justified in saying that he is "one with the Father"—a phrase not applied to any human being in the Hebrew Scriptures.[3]

Jesus' view of God is clearly monotheistic, not pantheistic. "At the beginning the Creator 'made them male and female,'" he declares (Matthew 19:4). Jesus refers to God as a transcendent moral agent, a being who acts according to his own aims. After Jesus frees a man plagued by a legion of demons, he admonishes him, "Return home and tell how much God has done for you" (Luke 8:39). God was responsible for the man's liberation. God acts morally and personally. Jesus addresses God as "our Father" in the Lord's prayer (Matthew 6:9). The very act of praying assumes a personal and knowing being who hears and responds to prayer. Unlike some Eastern worldviews that emphasize contemplating or meditating on one's own essence (or lack thereof, in the case of Buddhism), Jesus emphasizes the practice of prayer to a God who can hear and make a difference in life and history (Mark 11:22-25; Luke 11:1-13; 18:1-14). He affirms the value of worship to God on the same theological basis (John 4:24).

Jesus also affirms that God is holy or righteous. These words have lost their significance for many today. For an ancient Jew, they meant moral impeccability, perfection, and freedom from corruption. God is holy and commands his people to be holy (Leviticus 19:2). Jesus echoes this when he admonishes, "Be perfect, therefore, as your heavenly Father is perfect" (Matthew 5:48). He also addresses God as "Holy Father" (John 17:11) and "Righteous Father" (John 17:25). For Jesus, God is the ultimate moral standard whose ways are right, just, and loving. Hence, Jesus instructs his disciples to pray, "hallowed be your name," when addressing their "Father in heaven" (Matthew 6:9).

Although divine transcendence—God's existence apart and distinct from the universe—is central to Jesus' conception of God's holiness, he also affirms the presence of God in creation and with God's children. God "sees what is done in secret" (Matthew 6:4, 6, 18). Jesus' statement that "the kingdom of God is within you" (Luke 17:21) means that God's dynamic rule is present in the midst of Jesus' own ministry.[4] God's kingdom is not entirely beyond this world or limited to its future manifestations. God is "Lord of heaven and earth" (Luke 10:21). Using an *a fortiori* argument, Jesus makes this promise concerning divine immanence in the lives of people who seek God:

> Which of you fathers, if your children ask for a fish, will give them a snake instead? Or if they ask for an egg, will give them a scorpion? If you then, though you are evil, know how to give good gifts to your children, how much more will your Father in heaven give the Holy Spirit to those who ask him! (Luke 11:11-13).

Jesus pledges to his disciples that when they are persecuted by religious and political authorities, "the Holy Spirit will teach you at that time what you should say" (Luke 12:12). They would not be alone in their trials. Jesus counsels his followers not to worry about their lives because if God cares for the birds and flowers God will certainly provide for his more valuable creatures, especially if they seek first his kingdom (Matthew 6:25-34). This teaching assumes God's active and benevolent presence in all creation and in human affairs. Jesus illustrates the love of God and the importance of prayer in his parable of the persistent widow. A judge who didn't fear God or care about people was persistently approached by a widow seeking justice against her adversary. She was so persistent that the judge relented and granted her request—not for moral reasons, but because she was irritating him.

Jesus again argues *a fortiori* and says, "And will not God bring about justice for his chosen ones, who cry out to him day and night? Will he keep putting them off?" (Luke 18:1-7).

God's benevolent concern is even more directly stated when Jesus announces that "God so loved the world that he gave his one and only Son, that whoever believes in him shall not perish but have eternal life" (John 3:16). Instead of merely speaking of general providence, Jesus calls attention to God's specific and loving actions as revealed in his Son. In so doing, Jesus associates his very identity as "the Son" with God's loving purpose for salvation. By the same token, he prays that his followers might "be brought to complete unity to let the world know that you [the Father] sent me and have loved them even as you have loved me" (John 17:23).

Although the concept of the Trinity is more developed in the rest of the New Testament (and later formalized in the church's creeds), Jesus did intimate the notion of one God as triune when he authorized his disciples to baptize in the name of the Father, the Son, and the Holy Spirit (Matthew 28:19). Jesus prays to God the Father, speaks of the Holy Spirit in ontologically exalted terms (John 14:26), and affirms his own equality with God (John 8:58)[5]—all without ever speaking of more than one God.[6]

Jesus' View of Humanity

Jesus' affirmation of the metaphysical distinction between the Creator and the creation undergirds all his teachings about how humans ought to relate to God in service, worship, work, prayer, faith, and more. Jesus teaches that women and men are of great worth as God's creatures. They are "more valuable" than the birds of the air (Matthew 6:26; 10:31). This and similar statements are rooted in the Hebrew understanding that humans are made in God's image and likeness, and have been given charge over creation (Genesis 1:26-28; 5:1-2; Psalm 8). The worth of humans is also presumed in Jesus' statement of the golden rule. We ought to treat others as we would have them treat us, since all people are worthy of respect and love (Matthew 7:12).

Jesus reckons people as valuable spiritual beings, who, nonetheless, can betray their own selves through spiritual error. "What good will it be for you to gain the whole world, yet forfeit your soul? Or what can you give in exchange for your soul"? (Matthew 16:26). The human person is of incomparable worth; nothing can be exchanged for it, and its loss is catastrophic. "Do not be afraid of those who kill the body but cannot kill the soul. Rather, be afraid of the One who can destroy both soul and body in hell" (Matthew 10:28). Kant's view that humans should never be treated merely as means but always as ends in themselves is in fundamental agreement with Jesus.

Jesus' anthropology distinguishes the soul from the body. Some have claimed that any kind of mind-body dualism is rooted in Greek metaphysics, not Hebrew theology. Although there are differences between Greek dualism and biblical thought, many passages from the Hebrew Bible and other Jewish literature speak of the soul's separation from the body at death.[7] Numerous statements by Jesus affirm the ontological distinction of soul and body, as does the one just cited (Matthew 10:28). Jesus said to his disciples shortly before his arrest, "Watch and pray so that you will not fall into temptation. The spirit is willing, but the body is weak" (Matthew 26:41). He drew a distinction between two aspects of the person, which are interrelated but not identical or reducible to one another. The charge, "Watch and pray," assumes that one has some mental control over the weaknesses of the body, and thus that mind and body are not identical.[8] When Jesus promises the criminal crucified at his side that "today you will be with me in paradise" (Luke 23:43), he could not be referring to their physical bodies, since both would soon die and be buried. They would be together as spirits in the spiritual realm. Elsewhere Jesus argues from Scripture that Abraham, Isaac, and Jacob were still spiritually alive when God appeared to Moses in the burning bush, although they had long ago physically died (Matthew 22:29-32).

It is true that Jesus'—and other biblical writers'—use of the word translated "soul" (either in Hebrew or Greek) can sometimes refer to the entirety of one's life (mental and physical), but there are significant passages where "soul" speaks of an immaterial aspect of the person not identified with one's physical body. This aspect of the person survives physical death.[9]

Jesus' anthropology is therefore incompatible with that of idealists and pantheists who claim there is no physical reality. It is also incompatible with Gnostic dualism. The Jesus presented in the non-canonical Gnostic documents teaches that the bodily realm must be transcended in order to attain gnosis (esoteric knowledge of one's spiritual essence). This highlights a strong dualism between the spiritual realm taken to be good, and the physical realm reckoned as evil or debased. One's materiality is not the result of a good Creator's will, but of a lesser deity's cosmic mistake. This cosmic error must be overcome through knowledge of one's own spiritual essence.

The Jesus of the Gospels, however, affirms the Jewish theology of the original goodness of God's creation, both physical and spiritual. However far humans may fall short ethically and spiritually, their essential problem is not that they are imprisoned in matter, but that they fail to rightly honor and worship their good Creator.[10]

Neither can Jesus' view of humanity be squared with materialists or physicalists who deny the reality of an immaterial soul. Jesus' teaching is also unlike Buddhist teachings that the self is not a real and substantial entity, but a collection of disparate and bundled states that separate at death. Jesus' philosophy of personal identity is that human nature is a substance or essence that endures through time and survives even physical death. This is because human persons are created by a personal God who insures the human person's metaphysical integrity through change. However, Jesus taught that the disembodied state is not eternal. The soul and body would be reunited at the resurrection of the dead.

The mind-body debate has long raged in philosophy, and several versions of materialism or physicalism have gained ground in the West since the Enlightenment. Nevertheless, a significant number of contemporary philosophers defend forms of mind-body dualism. From a larger perspective, if naturalism as a worldview is questionable and if good arguments can be given for God's existence, the existence of the soul becomes much more credible.[11] Jesus, however, does not advance conjectural arguments about the soul. He either reasons from Scripture or makes claims based on his own supernatural credentials on this subject.

Jesus' teaching on the soul has an epistemological implication about the soul's capacity to know and experience God. Because God is also a personal, relational, and spiritual reality with an enduring identity, God can be known in various ways by human persons.[12]

While humans have an inestimable importance to Jesus, he sees them as tragically flawed, both morally and spiritually. The soul is in a perilous position before the expanse of eternity. During a discussion about what makes a person "unclean," or defiled before God's holiness, Jesus zeroes in on what he takes to be the inner dynamic.

> What comes out of you is what makes you "unclean." For from within, out of your hearts, come evil thoughts, sexual immorality, theft, murder, adultery, greed, malice, deceit, lewdness, envy, slander, arrogance and folly. All these evils come from inside and make you "unclean" (Mark 7:20-23).

The term "heart" refers to the core of one's mental and moral being, not merely to the emotions. It identifies the motivating essence of a person. Jesus connects one's inner life with one's final status before God.

> Good people bring good things out of the good stored up in them, and evil people bring evil things out of the evil stored up in them. But I tell you that people will have to give account on the day of judgment for every careless word they have spoken. For by your words you will be acquitted, and by your words you will be condemned (Matthew 12:35-37).

Jesus regards human sin not as an occasional mistake, but as a deep-rooted proclivity to resist the ways of God. "I tell you the truth, everyone who sins is a slave to sin" (John 8:34). Jesus reproaches the most well-informed and serious religious leaders of his day, proclaiming that "not one of you keeps the [moral] law" (John 7:19). Jesus' message is to those who recognize their need: "I have not come to call the righteous, but sinners to repentance" (Luke 5:31-32). In this, he reflects and continues the tradition of the Hebrew prophets, who often called Israel back to God by exposing people's inner corruption.[13]

It should be noted that Jesus' assessment of sin before God is far removed from the idea of karma, which is an impersonal law of cause and effect regarding the outcomes of human (and even nonhuman) actions over successive lifetimes. Jesus always relates the human condition to the realities of a personal and moral God, not to an abstract or cosmic principle of retribution or reward. He did not teach reincarnation, but the resurrection of the dead (John 5:28-29; see also Hebrews 9:27).

Jesus on Supernatural Beings

Like many of his contemporary Jews (but unlike the Sadducees), Jesus believed in angels and demons. The Gospels frequently describe Jesus expelling demons from various people plagued by their presence. The Gospels describe these supernatural entities as having mind, will, and emotion. Jesus dispatches them without ceremony, incantation, ritual, or struggle. He simply bids them to leave, sometimes after a brief conversation. Jesus also speaks of Satan or the devil in several passages, although he converses far more about God, God's kingdom, and discipleship. Jesus describes Satan as "the evil one" (Matthew

6:13) and the leader of demons (Matthew 25:41), whose nature is to lie, kill, destroy, and deceive (John 8:44; 10:10). He evinces no fear of Satan or of demons.

But Jesus is no polytheist or animist. Angels, demons and Satan are not divine or demigods, but creatures. Nor is Jesus a metaphysical dualist who envisions a struggle between equally powerful but opposing spiritual forces locked in eternal and irresolvable combat. Rather, he speaks of "the eternal fire prepared for the devil and his angels" (Matthew 25:41). Their rebellion is ultimately futile. The Gospels of Matthew and Luke record Jesus overcoming the temptations of Satan in the wilderness (Matthew 4:1-11; Luke 4:1-13).

Angels appear in connection with Jesus' ministry several times (Mathew 4:11; Luke 22:39-43). In his teaching, Jesus occasionally alludes to angels—powerful but finite spiritual beings who do not sin and are obedient to God's purposes (Matthew 18:10; 22:30). The Hebrew Scriptures also refer to these spiritual creatures as under God's command (Psalm 34:7; 148:2; Daniel 6:22). Tellingly, Jesus predicts a time at "the end of the age" when "the Son of Man will send out *his* angels, and they will weed out of his kingdom everything that causes sin and all who do evil" (Matthew 13:40-41, emphasis added; Mark 13:26-27). The angels are under the command of Jesus (the Son of Man), which closely identifies Jesus with the very being of God.

The subject of angels and demons has not received much attention in modern philosophy, although there is plenty of material on supernatural beings up through medieval philosophy and even now in theology, biblical studies, and popular culture. Contemporary philosopher Mortimer Adler (d. 2001) treats the subject philosophically in a recent volume and concludes that the subject of angels is important and that the existence of angels is not philosophically untenable.[14] Materialists or physicalists rule out the possibility of purely spiritual beings *a priori*; others question the notion of disembodied agents. These questions are closely related to the mind-body problem. If solid arguments are given for an immaterial substance in humans, then the existence of angels—disembodied beings—becomes less logically troublesome.

Jesus on History and the Afterlife

Jesus speaks of God as both the Creator of the world and the sovereign of history. He often refers to divinely-orchestrated events in the history of the Jewish people as illustrating moral and spiritual

Jesus' Metaphysics

truths. He heralds the coming of a new chapter in the kingdom of God as demonstrated in his own teaching, preaching, and ministry.

Generally speaking, for Jesus, the kingdom of God indicates God's intervention in history to accomplish both redemption and judgment. The kingdom refers to God's authority and dominion, rather than a set location or one group of people. Jesus refers to the kingdom having both present and future dimensions; it is breaking forth in the actions of Jesus, but much more is yet to come.

First and foremost, Jesus connects the coming of the kingdom in a new and unprecedented way with his own identity and mission. As biblical scholar F. F. Bruce put it:

> In Origen's great word, Jesus was the *autobasileia*, the kingdom in person; for the principles of the kingdom of God could not have been more completely embodied than in him who said to his Father, "not my will, but thine be done," and accepted the cross in that spirit.[15]

Jesus claims that his authority over the spiritual realm serves as evidence that the kingdom of God has come (Matthew 12:28).

Before Jesus explains the significance of the parable of the sower, he says to his disciples that "the knowledge of the secrets of the kingdom of heaven has been given to you."

> Blessed are your eyes because they see, and your ears because they hear. For I tell you the truth, many prophets and righteous people longed to see what you see but did not see it, and to hear what you hear but did not hear it (Matthew 13:1-17).

This reality of the kingdom is resident in the person and actions of Jesus, although many, Jesus laments, do not apprehend it.

Second, the kingdom of God is not limited to the Jewish nation, but is offered broadly, even to Gentiles (Luke 13:29-30). In fact, many Jews would fail to recognize the coming of the kingdom in Jesus and so would forfeit its benefits (Luke 14:15-24). This claim of God's universal purposes beyond the Jews scandalized many in Jesus' audiences.

Third, Jesus views the kingdom of God and the flow of history as intimately related to his own ongoing and perpetual authority. After his resurrection, Jesus announces:

All authority in heaven and on earth has been given to me. Therefore go and make disciples of all nations, baptizing them in the name of the Father and of the Son and of the Holy Spirit, and teaching them to obey everything I have commanded you. And surely I am with you always, to the very end of the age (Matthew 28:18-20).

Jesus also tells his disciples that they will receive the power through the Holy Spirit to be his witnesses "in Jerusalem, and in all Judea and Samaria, and to the ends of the earth" (Acts 1:8).

In light of the postmodernist criticism of "totalizing metanarratives" (worldviews claiming objective and universal truth) as intrinsically unjust, one should observe that Jesus commissions his followers to persuade and influence people through teaching that is empowered by the Holy Spirit. He never authorizes imperialism, exploitation, coercion, threats, or any other means of illicit power over others. Instead, he tells us to love our neighbors and even our enemies (Matthew 5:43-48). The Book of Acts shows the early Christians winning conversions through persuasion, not coercion or manipulation. Sadly, some later Christians who held the reigns of political power did enforce Christian conformity through the sword. One would be hard pressed, though, to find any warrant for this in the teachings of Jesus (or the Apostles).

Beyond history, Jesus speaks of a postmortem existence either with God in blessing or outside of God's blessing in a state of regret, loss, and forfeiture. Jesus announces to the criminal crucified next to him that the man would be with Jesus in paradise that very day (Luke 23:43). In the parable of Lazarus and the rich man, Jesus contrasts the beggar Lazarus, who "died and the angels carried him to Abraham's side," with the oppressive rich man who died and found himself in "hell, where he was in torment" (Luke 16:19-23). Jesus also warns of a day when he will separate the "sheep" from the "goats" eternally on the basis of how people lived their lives in response to him and to their neighbors (Matthew 25:31-46). Jesus implicitly builds on certain passages in the Hebrew Scriptures to this effect (Daniel 12:2; etc.), but he makes himself the key agent of eternal judgment.

Jesus teaches that one passes from death into a disembodied intermediate state—either into God's presence or away from it—and that at some future time this will be followed by Jesus' own return to earth in final judgment. After this the permanent resurrection of the body will occur.

46

> For a time is coming when all who are in their graves will hear his [the Son of God's] voice and come out—those who have done good will rise to live, and those who have done evil will rise to be condemned" (John 5:28-29).

Jesus claims to have the authority to render final judgment.

> Not everyone who says to me, 'Lord, Lord,' will enter the kingdom of heaven, but only those who do the will of my Father who is in heaven. Many will say to me on that day, 'Lord, Lord, did we not prophesy in your name, and in your name drive out demons and perform many miracles?' Then I will tell them plainly, 'I never knew you. Away from me, you evil doers' (Matthew 7:21-23).

Hell on Trial

Such statements by Jesus have led some to reject Jesus as a sound thinker or a moral teacher. Bertrand Russell in his famous essay, "Why I Am Not a Christian," is illustrative.

> There is one very serious defect to my mind in Christ's moral character, and that is that He believed in hell. I do not myself feel that any person who is really profoundly humane can believe in everlasting punishment.[16]

Russell claims that Jesus demonstrated "vindictive fury against those people who would not listen to His preaching." Moreover, Jesus' teaching that it is possible to sin against the Holy Spirit such that one is never forgiven "has caused an unspeakable amount of misery in the world." A kind person would never have unleashed such worries upon the world.[17] Furthermore, Jesus took "a certain pleasure in contemplating wailing and gnashing of teeth, or else it would not occur so often."[18] Lastly, Russell claims that the doctrine of hell "put cruelty into the world and gave the world generations of cruel torture; and the Christ of the Gospels, if you could take Him as his chroniclers represent Him, would certainly have to be considered partially responsible for that."[19] If Russell's charges stand, Jesus falls morally and philosophically. They may be questioned, however.

First, Jesus did not engage in "vindictive fury" when predicting divine judgment. He issues strong warnings at times, but shows no "pleasure in contemplating wailing and gnashing of teeth." Moreover, after pronouncing seven charges (or "woes") against "teachers of the law and Pharisees" (Matthew 23:15-32), Jesus *laments* over Jerusalem for not accepting his offer of redemption.

> O Jerusalem, Jerusalem, you who kill the prophets and stone those sent to you, how often I have longed to gather your children together, as a hen gathers her chicks under her wings, but you were not willing (Matthew 23:37).

While dying on the cross, Jesus prays concerning those responsible for his crucifixion, "Father, forgive them, for they do not know what they are doing" (Luke 23:34). This is not vindictive, but forgiving and compassionate. Rather than being spiteful, Jesus issues *warnings* precisely because he believes in both heaven and hell. That he warns of eternal loss repeatedly does not entail that he takes any enjoyment in it, any more than a physician enjoys repeatedly warning an asthmatic patient that she will die if she doesn't stop smoking. If Jesus did, in fact, believe that an eternal sin against the Holy Spirit were possible, it would only behoove him to warn others against committing it (Mark 3:20-30). The fact that some have worried unnecessarily about committing this sin should not be credited to Jesus any more than pathologists should be blamed when hypochondriacs think they have contracted diseases they do not have.

Second, Russell's claim that the very idea of hell induced generations to cruelly torture others is terribly overstated. We can cite a few Inquisitors who tortured heretics in hopes that early torment might spare them eternal punishment, but this is but a small and deeply aberrational percentage of Christians throughout the ages. The majority of those who purport to follow Jesus have adopted the attitude of warning and invitation with respect to Jesus' message of redemption, not the practice of torture. Torture is nowhere commended by the Jewish or Christian Scriptures (or any Christian Creed) as a method of conversion or purgation or retaliation.

Third, while some regard the very idea of hell as utterly repugnant, philosophical arguments have been marshaled in support of the doctrine of hell. If one can rationally support the idea of God's perfect and infinite holiness and justice in relation to the reality of human sin and moral responsibility, the idea of the perpetual punishment of one who rejects God's offer of redemption is not without warrant. As Milton's Lucifer put it in *Paradise Lost:*

> So farewell Hope, and with Hope farewell Fear,
> Farewell Remorse; all Good to me is lost;
> Evil be thou my Good. . . .
> Better to reign in Hell, than serve in Heav'n.[20]

Moreover, there are biblically tenable and philosophically defensible models of hell that are not vindictive at all.[21]

Jesus articulated a robust metaphysics. He embraced a highly personal theism and God's dominion over human and cosmic history, a dominion that was entering a new and decisive stage through his own ministry. Jesus was a mind-body dualist, who acknowledged the resurrection of the dead and eternal judgment. He often engaged the demonic realm through exorcism and healing, and he spoke of Satan, demons, and angels. However, his main focus was always on God and his own mandate "to seek and to save the lost" (Luke 19:10).

---

[1] Dwight Goddard, *A Buddhist Bible* (Boston: Beacon Press, 1938); quoted in Ian S. Markham, *A World Religions Reader*, 2nd ed. (Malden, MA: Blackwell Publishers, 2000), 131.

[2] See H.P. Owen, "Theism," in Paul Edwards, ed., *The Encyclopedia of Philosophy*, 8 vols. (New York: Macmillan and the Free Press, 1967) 8: 97. I have expanded on Owen's definition somewhat.

[3] See Douglas Groothuis, *Jesus in an Age of Controversy* (Eastbourne, UK: Kingsway Publications, 1998), 228-230.

[4] Alternative translations for Luke 17:11 are "the kingdom of God is in your midst" or "the kingdom of God is among you."

[5] Jesus' claims to deity will be discussed in chapter eight.

[6] On the theology and philosophy of the Trinity, see Millard Erickson, *God in Three Persons* (Grand Rapids, MI: Baker Books, 1995).

[7] Such as Ecclesiastes 12:6-7; Isaiah 10:18; 38:10, 12, 17.

[8] Paul K. Moser, "Jesus on the Knowledge of God," *Christian Scholar's Review* XXVII, no. 4 (1999): 588.

[9] See also Mark 9:2-10; Matthew 17:1-9; Luke 9:28-36; John 11:26; and Moser, 586-591. See John W. Cooper, *Body, Soul, and the Life Everlasting: Biblical Anthropology and the Monism-Dualism Debate* (Grand Rapids, MI, William B. Eerdmans Publishing Company, 1989).

[10] See Groothuis, *Jesus*, 77-101.

[11] See J.P. Moreland, *Scaling the Secular City* (Grand Rapids, MI: Baker Books, 1987), especially chapters 1-4.

[12] See Moser, 591.

[13] See Jeremiah 17:9; Isaiah 6:1-8.

[14] Mortimer Adler, *The Angels and Us* (New York: MacMillan Publishers, Co, Inc., 1982).

[15] F. F. Bruce, *New Testament History (Garden* City: NY: Doubleday, 1972), 173; emphasis in the original.

[16] Bertrand Russell, *Why I am Not a Christian and Other Essays on Religion and Related Subjects* (New York: Simon and Schuster, 1957), 17.

[17] Ibid., 12-13.

[18] Ibid., 18.

[19] Ibid.

[20] While Milton's Lucifer captures the essence of unmitigated rebellion against divine authority, the concept of "reigning in hell" is incoherent, since the biblical concept of hell allows for no such relationship between persons. Hell has no real rewards.

[21] See Michael J. Murray, "Heaven and Hell," in Michael J. Murray, ed., *Reason for the Hope Within* (Grand Rapids, MI: Eerdmans, 1999), 287-317; and C.S. Lewis' chapter, "Hell," in *The Problem of Pain* (New York: Simon and Schuster, 1996; orig. pub. 1962), 105-114.

5

Jesus' Epistemology

Epistemology is the philosophical pursuit occupied with the rational appraisal of truth-claims. It addresses the sources, standards, means, and scope of knowledge. The words "Jesus" and "epistemology" are not often brought together. Yet Jesus had convictions about how we acquire knowledge, even if his epistemology was more implicit than explicit. He did not fret about skepticism or the justification of our knowledge of the external world. He would often invoke the reality of the external world to make various theological and moral points—as when he tells religious leaders that while they can understand weather patterns, they "cannot interpret the signs of the times" (Matthew 16:3). In this, he is a common sense realist. Jesus often marshals empirical evidence to support his claims. He also regards noncontradiction and existential viability as tests for truth, and emphasizes the importance of imagination and character for knowing in the context of God's revelation.

Factual Evidence

Although Jesus speaks often of the spiritual realm beyond what is strictly observable, he also maintains that empirical evidence is available for many of his affirmations.[1] Jesus always assumes that one's beliefs ought to fit the facts. To believe in his teachings does not mystically remove one from the world of time and space and events. In various contexts, Jesus presented himself as the fulfillment of the Hebrew Scriptures' anticipation of the Messiah (see Luke 24:13-49).[2] When John the Baptist questioned Jesus' legitimacy, Jesus appealed to the evidence of his work to support his claim to be the Messiah (Matthew 11:4-6). He called people to believe in him on the basis of his signs or miracles, the extraordinary character of which helped established his authority (John 10:38). Jesus repeatedly argued that his interpretations of the Scriptures—concerning the Sabbath, the Messiah, religious obligations, and so on—better fit the facts than those of his critics.

Jesus predicted that he would be executed and would rise from the dead "on the third day"—a specific, datable time—and would reconnect with his disciples on earth (Matthew 16:21). The Gospels present Jesus as eating food and being empirically observable after the resurrection. Jesus invites his disciples to "Look at my hands and my feet. It is I myself! Touch me and see" (Luke 24:39).[3] The Apostle John's testimony amplifies this empirical dimension: "That which was from the beginning, which we have heard, which we have seen with our eyes, which we have looked at and our hands have touched—this we proclaim concerning the Word of life" (1 John 1:1). Jesus also predicts a time when he will return after his resurrection in a manner that is unmistakable to all (Mark 13:26).

Concerning ethics, Jesus teaches that one's character is assessed (at least in part) by empirical evidence: "Thus, by their fruit you will recognize them" (Matthew 7:20). He also asks, "Why do you call me, 'Lord, Lord,' and do not do what I say?" (Luke 6:46). Facts may falsify words.

Noncontradiction as a Test for Truth

Jesus reasons from the Scriptures and he reasons against his critics. When presented with an apparently irresolvable dilemma concerning the resurrected state or political allegiance (Matthew 22:15-22), he finds a *tertium quid* that avoids either horn of the dilemma. In this, and all his other use of argument, Jesus implicitly endorses the law of noncontradiction as a necessary test for truth. A statement and its negation cannot both be true in the same way at the same time. Jesus never accepts a proposition and its negation as both true; nor does he revel in irreconcilable paradoxes as a way to disarm rational thought and make room for faith. Jesus at no time invokes an irresolvable paradox when pressed into a logical corner—although he will often employ a paradox to give a memorable ending to a pertinent teaching. When accused of holding contradictory teachings or of opposing the Hebrew Scriptures, Jesus argues in order to resolve the apparent contradiction and vindicate his teaching.

Nevertheless, some interpreters attempt to make Jesus into a

52

Jewish Zen-Master or guru by claiming that he employed mind-stopping contradictions. They compare several paradoxical sayings of Jesus to Zen koans. A koan is a riddle having to do with a logical impossibility; it is given to a Zen student in order to induce the student to transcend normal logical analysis and rational processes. Zen epistemology involves transcending all dualities and antitheses through various practices, such as contemplating koans and sat-zen (meditating on a blank wall for hours) in order to attain the state of "no-mind." A famous Zen koan is, "What is the sound of one hand [clapping]?" This question has no resolution, because one hand cannot clap (in any standard sense of clapping).[4]

Jesus utters statements that are *prima facie* similar to koans, such as, "But many who are first will be last, and many who are last will be first (Matthew 19:30). But Jesus' use of paradox is pedagogical, not illogical. It has nothing to do with Zen or any other kind of mystical practice that abandons rational categories as a means to enlightenment. Jesus' paradoxes are given not as epigrams, but as memorable conclusions to his teachings. They have an intellectual context and communicate propositional knowledge. The statement, "Many who are first will be last, and many who are last will be first" is not affirming that "first equals last" (a contradiction), as would a Zen koan. Rather, Jesus is speaking of the final reward of those who give up much in this life to follow him. This reward more than compensates for the losses they experience. Therefore, many who are "first" (or fortunate in this life) will be "last" (or unfortunate in the next), and vice versa. Jesus' phrasing is paradoxical, and, therefore, pedagogically provocative; but it has a determinative and intelligible meaning (see Matthew 19:16-30).

The Existential Effects of Knowledge

Jesus did not hold a pragmatic definition of truth. He did not think that what *made* a statement true was whether or not it produced a desirable or beneficial effect. In that case, he would have left the self-satisfied Pharisees and theologically aberrant Sadducees (who denied the afterlife) alone with "their own truth." On the contrary, Jesus said things like: "Stop judging by mere appearances, and make a right judgment" (John 7:24). Right judgments must match reality as it is; they must fit the facts.

Nevertheless, Jesus claimed that his teachings were applicable and practical—that they had beneficial consequences in this life and certainly in the next—despite the personal sacrifices that he warned would be required from his adherents. This indicates the practical or existential test for truth. If Jesus' teachings are true, they should concretely relate to life and produce a better manner of living, of human flourishing, than otherwise possible. That is, they must be existentially viable.[5] The Sermon on the Mount ends with a mini-parable to this effect.

> Therefore, everyone who hears these words of mine and puts them into practice is like a wise man who built his house on the rock. The rain came down, the streams rose, and the winds blew and beat against that house; yet it did not fall, because it had its foundation on the rock. But everyone who hears these words of mine and does not put them into practice is like a foolish man who built his house on sand. The rain came down, the streams rose, and the winds blew and beat against that house, and it fell with a great crash (Matthew 7:24-27).

Jesus further taught that his followers would experience a definite transformation in their lives: "The thief comes only to steal and kill and destroy; I have come that they may have life, and have it to the full" (John 10:10). In many passages, Jesus assures his followers that certain desirable spiritual changes will occur in their characters as a result of following him. Despite trials, persecutions, self-denial, and other consequences of discipleship, they will not walk in darkness, be alone, or be overcome by anything (Matthew 28:20; Luke 21:10-19).

Knowledge and Imagination: Parables

Jesus' frequent use of parables has epistemological implications. The meaning of Jesus' parables has been much discussed, but our focus will be on the importance of these fictional (but truth-conveying) stories in Jesus' theory of knowledge.[6]

Like the Hebrew prophets before him, much of Jesus' teaching is parabolic, as opposed to discursive. He uses parables most often to explain the kingdom and character of God. But a parable is no less rational for not being discursive. It invites one to see logical relations in a dramatic form. The history of philosophy offers many memorable parables, most notably Plato's allegory of the cave from *The Republic*, where the prisoners mistake shadows for reality. Kierkegaard's writings are saturated with parables.[7]

Jesus' parables are fairly short and involve only a few characters. They engage listeners and challenge them to respond to and interpret the story for themselves. Jesus tells parables for various reasons, often using them to draw his hearers into a line of thought that would not otherwise be accessible. Although Jesus' parables have been interpreted allegorically in a grandiose fashion, their meaning should be taken from their context. Each parable has one or only a few main points and should not be pressed beyond that.

Jesus sometimes tells a parable instead of answering a question in a direct manner. This is because the questioner is asking the wrong question or would not listen to an argument. The famous parable of the Good Samaritan not only teaches several moral lessons, but also displays Jesus' concern for the imagination in the epistemology of moral knowledge.

An expert in the Jewish Law asks Jesus what must be done to inherit eternal life. Jesus asks the man what the Law says. The man answers that one must love God with all one's being, and love one's neighbor as oneself. Jesus responds that this is correct, and that if one does this, one would live. Luke tells us the man "wanted to justify himself," so he asks Jesus, "And who is my neighbor?" (Luke 10:25-29).

Instead of answering the question directly, Jesus tells the famous story of the man who was mugged while going from Jerusalem to Jericho and was left naked and half dead on the road. Both a priest and a Levite, people of high social and religious standing, passed by the poor man and did nothing. But a Samaritan took pity on the hapless fellow. He bandaged his wounds and carried him on his donkey to an inn where he had the innkeeper take care of the victim. The Samaritan picked up the bill. Then Jesus probes, "Which of these three do you think was a neighbor to the man who fell into the hands of robbers?" The expert responds, "The one who had mercy on him." Jesus replies, "Go and do likewise" (Luke 10:26-37).

Using a Samaritan as a hero was subversive, since Jews despised Samaritans as religious and racial half-breeds (see John 4:9). Instead of giving an abstract principle, such as "everyone is your neighbor," Jesus tells a parable in order to draw the man into the story and to redirect his thinking through the moral imagination. Jesus does not answer the man's question, "Who is my neighbor?" by saying, "You should be a neighbor to anyone in need." Rather, he changes the question to, "Who is a true neighbor to those in need?" He presents a scenario where a social outcast becomes a moral hero, while those with social status are callous and uncaring. The effect of this parable is to heighten the questioner's awareness of the demands of the moral Law and to expose any false pretense to righteousness.

In the parable of the tenants, Jesus tells a story in order to reveal how Israel has treated God's prophets. A man built a walled vineyard with a tower, then rented it to farmers before leaving on a journey. At harvest time, he sent a servant to collect some of the harvest as rent, but the tenants beat him and sent him away empty-handed. The owner dispatched another servant who was similarly abused. He then sent several others, who were either killed or beaten. Finally the only one left to send was the owner's son, whom he loved. "They will respect my son," he wrongly thought. The tenants realized this was the heir to the property, and said, "Come let's kill him, and the inheritance will be ours." So he, too, met his demise at their hands and was thrown out of the vineyard. Then Jesus said:

> What then will the owner of the vineyard do? He will come and kill those tenants and give the vineyard to others. Haven't you read this scripture: "The stone the builders rejected has become the capstone; the Lord has done this, and it is marvelous in our eyes"? (Mark 12:1-11; see Psalm 118:22-23).

Mark writes that the chief priests, the teachers of the law and the elders then "looked for a way to arrest him because they knew he had spoken the parable against them" (v. 12). They were indicted and convicted by Jesus' words.

Jesus had disputed matters of doctrine and ethics with these leaders for some time, but now, instead of giving another argument in his own defense, he implicates them as the faithless and cruel tenants who have failed to respect God's prophets or even God's own Son, Jesus himself. Jesus apparently did not explain who the characters in his parable represented. He let his audience discern that themselves, which is one reason why they were so agitated. They probably knew that Jesus was alluding to Isaiah 5:1-7, where Israel is portrayed as a vineyard that betrays God, its benevolent owner.

Jesus' use of parables serves many purposes, which are too varied to treat here. But the epistemological point is that they existentially draw the listener into the drama; they engage the imagination, clear the mind, spark the conscience, and challenge the will. Instead of being third-person discourses, they engender first-person participation.

They are not merely stories to enjoy. They hold up one reality to serve as a mirror of another, the kingdom of God. They are avenues to understanding, handles by which one can grasp the kingdom. Jesus told parables to confront people with the character of God's kingdom and to invite them to participate in it and to live in accordance with it.[8]

Here a legitimate contrast can be drawn between the Hebraic understanding of knowledge (which Jesus shared) and that of the ancient Greeks. Although both viewed truth as necessarily involving a correspondence with reality, in Greek thought, knowing God meant contemplating the ultimate reality as an unchanging philosophical abstraction. As C. H. Dodd put it:

> While the Greek knowledge of God is the most highly abstract form of pure contemplation, for the Hebrew it is essentially intercourse with God; it is to experience His dealing with men in time, and to hear and obey His commands.[9]

Jesus' emphasis on relational knowledge contrasts sharply with the Jesus of the Gnostic documents, who claims that spiritual knowledge (*gnosis*) is mystical contact with another world that leaves this world—as a space, time, historical reality—essentially untouched. *Gnosis* is an ineffable experience of something that transcends the corrupt and unredeemable material universe. For the Gnostics, the ultimate reality to be known is not the personal Creator and covenanting Lord of the Hebrew Scriptures, but a fullness (*pleroma*) beyond concepts and language and history. Therefore, Gnostic epistemology is entirely different from the way of knowing that Jesus presents in the canonical Gospels.[10]

Jesus tells parables for the purpose of opening his listeners' hearts to the Creator God who acts in history. His teachings call for decision and action. He never left his audience thinking, "That's an interesting idea. But what of it?" The parables are not entertainment.

The parable of the sower, however, condemns those who are blind, deaf, and hardhearted. Rather than stimulating those interested to further investigation, this parable pronounces a sentence of doom on the incorrigible (Matthew 13:1-15).

Character and Knowledge of God

In recent years, philosophers have begun to rediscover the role of moral character in epistemology. Philosophers still rightly ask what makes *beliefs* qualify as knowledge (truth plus justification or warrant), but more philosophers are now asking what makes *believers* good candidates for knowledge. What qualities best suit a person for attaining knowledge? What traits taint a person's capacity to know what ought to be known? This is called virtue epistemology; it has a long pedigree going back to Aquinas and Augustine in the Western tradition. Intellectual virtues have classically included qualities such as patience, tenacity, humility, studiousness, and honest truth-seeking. Vices to be avoided include impatience, gullibility, pride, vain curiosity, and intellectual apathy.[11]

There is a strong emphasis on character—both virtue and vice—in Jesus' epistemology, which is closely intertwined with his teachings on ethics and the knowledge of God. He not only gives arguments and tells parables, he calls people to intellectual rectitude and sobriety. Jesus' familiar moral teaching about the dangers of judgmentalism contains an epistemological element easily overlooked.

> Do not judge, or you too will be judged. For in the same way as you judge others, you will be judged, and with the measure you use, it will be measured to you. Why do you look at the speck of sawdust in someone else's eye and pay no attention to the plank in your own eye? How can you say, "Let me take the speck out of your eye," when all the time there is a plank in your own eye? You hypocrite, first take the plank out of your own eye, and then you will see clearly to remove the speck from the other person's eye (Matthew 7:1-5).

This passage is often taken out of context to forbid all moral evaluation, as if Jesus were a relativist. But Jesus has something else in mind: a clear-sighted self-evaluation and a proper evaluation of others based on objective standards. Jesus stipulates that all moral judgments relate to the self as much as to the other. Therefore, when one judges others, one is implicitly bringing oneself under the same judgment. One will be measured by the same measurement one employs. In light of that, a person needs first to search her or his own being for any moral impurities and seriously address them ("take the plank out of your own eye"). Only then is one in a good epistemological and ethical position

to evaluate another, to "see clearly" the speck in someone else's eye.
If one fails to evaluate oneself by one's own standard, one cannot rightly discern the moral status of others. In other words, proper moral evaluation requires a knowledge of the self, and allows no special pleading. The hypocrite is not only morally deficient, but epistemologically off-base as well. By failing to be subjectively attentive to one's conscience, one fails to discern moral realities objectively. Thus people will often condemn others overly because they ignore or obscure their own transgressions.

Jesus gives further incentive to evaluate situations justly—that is, to be virtuous knowers—when he warns that people will be held accountable before God for every word they utter. Their judgments issue from their character, and their character will affect their destiny.

> Good people bring good things out of the good stored up in them, and evil people bring evil things out of the evil stored up in them. But I tell you that people will have to give account on the day of judgment for every careless word they have spoken. For by your words you will be acquitted, and by your words you will be condemned (Matthew 12:35-37).

Jesus sometimes deemed the character of his hearers as interfering with their ability to know and apply the truth of his words and actions. In a quarrel over his own identity, Jesus accused his hearers of not understanding their own Scriptures or the testimony that John the Baptist gave on Jesus' behalf. Nor did they have "the love of God in their hearts."

> I have come in my Father's name, and you do not accept me; but if others come in their own names, you will accept them. How can you believe [in me] if you accept praise from one another, yet make no effort to obtain the praise that comes from the only God? (John 5:43-44).

One might think this is an *ad hominem* fallacy. Jesus is attacking the person, not the argument. But Jesus does not replace an argument with a negative assessment of character; rather, he explains their inability to believe in him according to their over-concern with social status, which precluded their seeking truth. Giving more evidence or arguments does not serve Jesus' purpose here; instead, he ferrets out their character defect and its epistemological consequences.

Jesus' Epistemology

While Jesus warns of vices that keep people from understanding his message, he also lauds certain virtues as conducive to spiritual knowledge, as when he says, "My teaching is not my own. It comes from him who sent me. Anyone who chooses to do the will of God will find out whether my teaching comes from God or whether I speak on my own" (John 7:16-17). A willingness to conform one's will to God's will is a requirement for discerning Jesus' authority in relation to "the Father"—a key to understanding Jesus' identity. He makes a comparable, though broader, statement in the Sermon on the Mount concerning persistence in seeking.

> Ask and it will be given to you; seek and you will find; knock and the door will be opened to you. For everyone who asks receives; he who seeks finds; and to him who knocks, the door will be opened (Matthew 7:7-8).

He similarly ties the knowledge that leads to freedom to whether or not one will be his disciple: "If you hold to my teaching, you are really my disciples. Then you will know the truth, and the truth will set you free" (John 8:31-32). Fidelity to Jesus leads to knowledge that liberates.

Yet in several cases, Jesus refuses to grant a sign or answer an argument because his hearers would not learn anything from such a response. They are not seeking truth, but resisting it. So he does not owe it to them. When pressed for a miraculous sign on demand, Jesus demurs and accuses his audience of being spiritually unfaithful (Matthew 16:1-4). A sign would have had no beneficial effect. Similarly, when Jesus is questioned as to his authority, he says he will answer only if his questioners say whether they take John the Baptist's activity to be from heaven or merely human. This sets up a dilemma from which they cannot escape. If they say John's authority is from God, Jesus will ask why they didn't follow John. If they say John's authority is only human, the crowds who rightly accept John as a prophet will reject them. "So they answered Jesus, 'We don't know.' Then he said, 'Neither will I tell you by what authority I am doing these things'" (Matthew 21:23-27). Jesus smoked out their presuppositions and forced a dilemma instead of providing an answer they would not have accepted anyway. In so doing, he uncovered their bad character that hindered their knowing.

Jesus' Knowledge of God

The root of Jesus' intellectual and spiritual confidence is his awareness of God's presence, power, promises, and pleasure. His trust in the Hebrew Scriptures as revelatory and authoritative (Matthew 5:17-20; John 10:35) confirms this orientation. God spoke through the Law and the prophets; and God continues to speak through Jesus himself. All four Gospels testify that Jesus spent long times in prayer, conversed with God, and lived out of an intense awareness of the divine will for his own life and for the entire cosmos. Since he knew the Father intimately, he was able to make the Father known to those who "have ears to hear and eyes to see."

A passage from Matthew (sounding much like Jesus' utterances in the Gospel of John) spotlights Jesus' relationship with God as the source of his knowledge.

> All things have been committed to me by my Father. No-one knows the Son except the Father, and no-one knows the Father except the Son and those to whom the Son chooses to reveal him (Matthew 11:27; see also John 10:15).

Jesus teaches in several places that some kinds of spiritual knowledge are only possible through God's revelatory activity. When Peter affirms the proposition that Jesus is "the Christ, the Son of the living God," Jesus announces that this truth was revealed to him "by my Father in heaven" (Matthew 16:13-17).

Still, Jesus exhorts people to reason, to reflect, and to seek. After the Matthew passage cited above, Jesus says, "Come to me, all you who are weary and burdened, and I will give you rest" (Matthew 11:28). Jesus' view of divine revelation did not preclude his invitation to all who would honestly investigate his teachings and his character. His view of divine initiative in revelation (and general providence) did not lead him to annul or minimize human responsibility regarding knowledge of the truths of this revelation.

Jesus and Religious Epistemology Today

Because few—if any—contemporary epistemologists of religion appeal to Jesus' theory of knowledge as a primary source for their own

61

epistemologies, it is difficult to relate Jesus' views to that of contemporary epistemology of religion. Nevertheless, I will venture a few suggestive comments.

An ongoing debate in the epistemology of religious belief concerns the rational justification of generic monotheism and Christian theism. To oversimplify somewhat, two distinct approaches dominate the field: that of Richard Swinburne and that of Alvin Plantinga, both well-respected philosophers. Swinburne offers a sustained case that belief in theism is justified on account of its logical coherence and the success of several inductive theistic arguments that render theism more plausible than nontheism. He claims that the specific historical claims of Christianity can also be defended by a careful appeal to cumulative evidences in their favor.[12] Plantinga, while not dismissing the value of theistic arguments, argues that belief in Christian theism can be "properly basic" and not based on other, more certain beliefs. A properly basic belief is self-certifying under certain conditions.[13] Christianity can be held rationally without the evidential chain of reasoning used by Swinburne, which Plantinga claims cannot give "warrant" (epistemological endorsement) to Christian belief because of its overall low probability.

Does Jesus' epistemology address this debate? Belief in the Creator appears to be a "properly basic belief" for Jesus—at least in the sense that he did not offer theistic arguments. For Jesus, theism was a master metaphysical principle from which he interpreted the world and his culture. Nevertheless, the Gospels never portray Jesus' theism as fideistic. He did not advocate belief in God through a sheer leap of rationally unjustified faith or merely on the basis of a mystical experience. Jesus' theism was the cornerstone of a well-integrated worldview. However, Jesus did not debate with atheists or skeptics, but with Jewish theists. He was never pressed to justify theism *per se*. That Jesus gave no theistic arguments, therefore, does not answer the questions as to whether (1) theists in other, more skeptical settings need to do so, or (2) whether these arguments might be successful philosophically.

However, in disputes over specific ethical and theological matters, Jesus cited evidence and marshaled arguments for his convictions. In these areas, he was not content to make specifically religious beliefs "properly basic" or presuppositional. When it came to Jesus' particular account of theism, he appealed to arguments and evidence more along the lines of Swinburne's project of religious justification.

One must remember that the task of arguing philosophically for

Jesus' Epistemology

the rationality of Christian belief two thousand years after the time of Jesus is quite different from Jesus' epistemological task as the very founder of Christianity. Nevertheless, keeping these two horizons in view may lead to some profitable philosophizing. Jesus had convictions about the sources, standards, and effects of knowledge. What one knows must fit the facts and be noncontradictory. Knowledge may come through nondiscursive and imaginative teachings, such as parables. One's character may impede or enhance knowledge. Who we are affects what we know. The knowledge Jesus imparts has, he claims, discernible effects on the entire person, in this world and in the next. Jesus' teachings issue from his own certainty of God's character.

---

[1] See also the discussion of Jesus' use of evidence in chapter three.

[2] Concerning Jesus' claims to fulfill messianic expectations, see Walter Kaiser, *The Messiah of the Old Testament* (Grand Rapids, MI: Zondervan, 1995).

[3] The issues surrounding the claim that Jesus rose from the dead are discussed in chapter eight.

[4] See William Johnston, *Christian Zen* (New York: Harper and Row, 1971), chapter seven, for the koan approach to Jesus and Christianity.

[5] This in no way implies that Jesus was an existentialist.

[6] On how fiction can communicate truth, see Michael Jubien, *Contemporary Metaphysics* (Malden, MA: Blackwell Publishers, 1997), 175-187.

[7] See Thomas C. Oden, ed. *The Parables of Kierkegaard,* reprint ed. (New York: Princeton University Press, 1989).

[8] K.R. Snodgrass, "Parable," in *Dictionary of Jesus and the Gospels*, ed. Joel B. Green, Scot McKnight, I. Howard Marshall (Downers Grove, IL: InterVarsity Press, 1992), 597.

[9] C.H. Dodd, *The Interpretation of the Fourth Gospel* (Cambridge: Cambridge University Press, 1953), 152.

[10] For more on Gnosticism, see Douglas Groothuis, *Jesus in an Age of Controversy* (Eastbourne, UK: Kingsway Publishers, 1998), 77-101.

[11] See Jay Wood, *Epistemology: Becoming Intellectually Virtuous* (Downers Grove, IL: InterVarsity Press, 1998).

[12] For an overview of Swinburne's approach, see his essay, "The Vocation of a Natural Theologian," in Kelly James Clark, ed. *Philosophers Who Believe* (Downers Grove, IL: InterVarsity Press, 1993), 179-202.

[13] See Alvin Plantinga, *Warranted Christian Belief* (New York: Oxford University Press, 2000).

63

6

The Ethics of Jesus

Jesus was not a social revolutionary or an academic lecturer on moral philosophy. He did start a movement, which became global and perpetual, but it was not a political or social movement *per se* (although Jesus has inspired numerous such movements). Instead, Jesus alerted his followers to the demands and privileges of God's kingdom. Neither was Jesus a sage who uttered metaphysical sayings or puzzles that detached one from everyday life, even though he spoke often of God and the afterlife.

Jesus enunciated an ethics of God's kingdom, so it is appropriate to relate his ethical teachings to his notion of God's dominion in history. After discussing Jesus' kingdom emphasis, we will address Jesus' ethics under the standard philosophical categories of virtue, deontology, and consequences. We will find that Jesus advocated determinate inner dispositions (virtues), loving obedience to rules of duty (deontology), and the production of morally good states of affairs (consequences). All three aspects must be held together to do justice to Jesus' approach.

Ethics for the Kingdom

Jesus stressed the immediacy and presence of the kingdom of God. He began his public teaching (echoing John the Baptist) by proclaiming, "Repent, for the kingdom of God is at hand" (Matthew 4:17). This conjoins ethical exhortation and theology. Jesus' charge to repent exhorts the whole person to turn toward Jesus and the kingdom of God; it is not a matter of minor moral reforms, etiquette, self-resolve, or positive thinking.

64

However, the reign and power of God are not completely manifested during Jesus' ministry. There is an "already, but not yet" tension to God's kingdom.[1] Therefore, Jesus teaches his disciples to pray, "Your kingdom come, your will be done" (Matthew 6:10). There is a future feast for those who find the kingdom (Matthew 22:1-14; Luke 14:15-24), as well as a future state of being that is entered into at the last judgment (Matthew 25:31-46). Jesus' ethical imperatives and sensibilities are couched within this present and future dynamic of God's redemptive dominion.

The Virtues of the Kingdom

Jesus is profoundly concerned with the character or inner disposition of people as they relate to God, others, and creation. He is not unlike the Hebrew prophets who often spoke of internal motivations and beliefs. Jesus' beatitudes stress attitudes that Jesus pronounces "blessed," or objectively good, right, and in harmony with God's ways. "Blessed" is not synonymous with our meaning of "happy"—a subjective state of pleasure or enjoyment. Jesus says that those who are "persecuted because of righteousness" are blessed (Matthew 5:10), as are "those who mourn" (Matthew 5:3). Therefore, mere happiness is not in view, but something deeper.

Jesus pronounces blessings and makes promises regarding: (1) the "poor in spirit"—another way of saying "humble," (2) "those who mourn"—who acknowledge their sin before God, (3) "the meek"— those humbly submitted to God, (4) "those who hunger and thirst for righteousness," (5) "the merciful," (6) "the pure in heart," (7) "the peace makers," and (8) those who are persecuted for doing good for the sake of Jesus (Matthew 5:1-11). Jesus blesses these actions and attitudes as intrinsically good before God, but each personal trait is also linked to a further benefit. For example, "Blessed are the meek, for they will inherit the earth." Paradoxically, meekness before God leads to possession of earthly enjoyment in the long haul. Likewise, those blessed with a pure heart "will see God."

Jesus' account of virtue is profoundly theological and teleological. Unlike a modern virtue theorist such as Iris Murdoch, who says we must be literally "good for nothing" (since there is no God, no afterlife, and no relationship between virtue and felicity),[2] Jesus places the virtues into a cosmic and supernatural framework, that of "blessedness." These character traits do not merely exhibit objective moral properties (Murdoch's view), they fit the world and the people

God has created. Jesus' account of virtue is similar to Aristotle's correlation of virtue and telos (cosmic purpose), where proper conduct is conducive to human flourishing. But Jesus' view is dissimilar as well, since Aristotle's philosophy allotted the Prime Mover no ethical role in establishing, announcing, or rewarding moral character. For Jesus, God is central to the nature and experience of virtue.

The Sermon on the Mount, from which the beatitudes are taken, repeatedly concentrates on the "heart"—which referred to the deepest and central reality of the person (not merely the emotional center). While Jesus does not set aside the Hebrew law, he radicalizes it and applies it in some disturbing ways. Jesus reminds his hearers that they have been taught, "Do not murder, and anyone who murders will be subject to judgment." But he goes beyond this to say, "Anyone who is angry with a brother or sister will be subject to judgment," as will anyone who uses abusive language against another. Therefore, one should make peace with others before giving religious offerings (Matthew 5:21-24). Jesus does not condemn all manner of anger, but the dangers intrinsic to anger, such as revenge, viciousness, and so on. Jesus himself unapologetically used a whip to clear the temple of its religious profiteering (John 2:14-22) and spoke harshly of religious hypocrisy (Matthew 23). In teaching people who already knew the moral law against committing adultery, Jesus adds, "But I tell you that anyone who looks at a woman lustfully has already committed adultery with her in his heart." Therefore, one should take radical action to avoid such harmful fantasies. Speaking hyperbolically, Jesus says to gouge out the offending eye and to cut off the offending hand (Matthew 5:27-30).

Philosopher Michael Martin rightly notes that "Jesus' emphasis on controlling one's thoughts, emotions, and desires has been de-emphasized and in many cases nearly eliminated from modern discussions of Christian ethics."[3] Yet he rejects these strictures as impractical and unwise, alleging that "if Jesus' injunction is interpreted as a command not to contemplate any evil actions at all, it has been maintained that it thwarts our imagination and forbids the contemplation of evil, for example, in art and literature." Martin thinks such contemplation really discourages evil instead of encouraging it.[4]

Jesus' injunctions against anger and lust should not be viewed as forbidding even the fictional portrayals of these emotions. Jesus' own parables describe wicked or foolish people who are not models of good character. Rather, Jesus' teaching disallows adopting an inner orientation that countenances, values or plays out the vices he mentions. Reading an account of an evil character in *The Brothers*

Karamazov, for example, would not violate Jesus' injunction. Wanting to emulate this character—or Milton's Lucifer—would violate Jesus' teachings, whether or not one ever acted out the imaginations.

Martin then considers whether Jesus' prohibition could be justified on the grounds that such angry or lustful thoughts might lead to actions involving deleterious consequences. He grants this is sometimes the case, as when "sexist language has indirectly harmful effects on women,"[5] but he discards Jesus' standards as too imposing and not warranted. Martin thinks that Jesus "may well have believed that certain thoughts or emotions were bad in themselves independent of their consequences."[6] Martin disagrees, because he deems consequences to be the determining factor in ethics. "Emotions, desires, thoughts, and feelings do not seem to be good or bad in themselves." [7]

Martin seems to have a utilitarian standard of moral evaluation in which the status of actions counts more than the character of persons. Utilitarianism is subject to many criticisms, but it suffices to say that many virtue theorists—Christian or otherwise—count certain inner states as having inherent moral value whether or not they produce actions, although in many cases they should produce actions. There is a moral obligation to be a particular kind of person, regardless of whether this results in external actions in every case. Virtues are more than dispositions to act, since they may obligate one to attain and maintain certain inner states or ways of being, which are good in themselves.[8] Jesus is not alone in his view of the moral status of inner states, although he puts his case more strongly than most contemporary ethicists would.

To illustrate the complementary view of virtue, consider which person you would rather have for a friend or would value more highly morally. William acts caring and respectful, but he entertains unduly angry thoughts toward you quite often, although never expresses them. George acts caring and loving to the same degree as William, but never has these angry thoughts about you. If you would pick George over William, Jesus' basic point is supported. Thoughts and attitudes do matter ethically.

Roger Scruton argues that sexual fantasizing is morally out of place because it devalues persons. Instead of deeming persons as objectively existing others, lust replaces persons with compliant images subject to one's arbitrary mental manipulation. "The fantasy blocks passage to reality." The "fantasy Other," who is completely the instrument of one's imagination, becomes merely an object to the one fantasizing. "The sexual world of the fantasist is a world without subjects, in which others appear as objects only."[9] Scruton argues that the very *mental act* of such fantasies is an exercise in unhealthy and disrespectful unreality. One might call it psychic rape. (Scruton believes that if the fantasist becomes possessed by this image, rape is the natural result.[10]) He thus provides a gloss on Jesus' own teaching— and a counterpoint to Martin's utilitarian, non-virtue approach.

Intrinsic to the blessed way of life that Jesus advocates is the virtue of humility. Blessed are the meek, the poor in spirit, and those who mourn. When Jesus discovers that his disciples had been bickering among themselves as to who was the greatest, he calls them to himself and says, "Anyone who wants to be first must be the very last, and the servant of all" (Mark 9:33-35). The humble don't wrangle over rating themselves against others, but find enjoyment, contentment, and meaning in service. Jesus offers humility through a relationship with his own humility: "Take my yoke upon you and learn from me, for I am gentle and humble in heart, and you will find rest for your souls" (Matthew 11:29). Jesus demonstrated this humility by washing his disciples' feet shortly before his crucifixion (John 13:1-11). In the Greco-Roman world of Jesus' day, humility was taken to be more of a vice than a virtue, a sign of weakness and failure. Frederick Nietzsche sounded similar themes in his thunderous criticisms of Christianity. Humility signals defeat; it is esteemed only as a psychological compensation for irretrievable loss. Only the losers believe that "the meek will inherit the earth." No, the earth will inherit the meek.

Against this, Jesus, the Hebrew prophets, and the entire Christian tradition finds in humility a well-adjusted and sober assessment of oneself in relation to God and others. It is rooted in both thanksgiving to God and in the awareness that one's endowments should be offered in loving service to one's neighbor (Matthew 22:37-40). Jesus' teachings on the future manifestation of the kingdom also reinforce the value of humility; it will be rewarded in the end. The antithesis of humility is the sin of pride, one of the seven deadly sins of the Western moral tradition. As Jesus said, "For those who exalt themselves will be humbled, and those who humble themselves will be exalted" (Matthew 23:12). After a conversation among the disciples as to who would be the most favored, Jesus teaches:

> You know that those who are regarded as rulers of the Gentiles lord it over them, and their high officials exercise authority over them. Not so with you. Instead, whoever wants to become great among you must be your servant, and whoever wants to be first must be slave of all. For even the Son of Man did not come to be

served, but to serve, and to give his life as a ransom for many (Mark 10:42-45).

Forgiveness plays a compelling role in Jesus' ethics of virtue, and is closely related to humility. The humble person will not hold a grudge or nurse an offense, but will forgive. Jesus even ties one's willingness to forgive others to being forgiven by God (Matthew 6:14-15) and counsels his followers to extend forgiveness to all who ask for it (Luke 17:3). We should ask God to forgive us even as we forgive others (Matthew 6:12). As one receives forgiveness from God and others, one should in turn offer forgiveness to others (Matthew 18:21-35). Unlike many popular psychological approaches, Jesus did not advise forgiving others the sake of one's mental, emotional, or physical health (however beneficial it may be), but saw forgiveness as an ethical duty expressing a virtue. Forgiveness is an attitude and action consonant with the objective realities of God as a forgiving God. Jesus modeled forgiveness while dying on the cross when he prayed, "Father forgive them, for they do not know what they are doing" (Luke 23:34).

Divine Duties: Deontology

One cannot easily make the division between deontology and virtue in the teachings of Jesus (or in the Scriptures as a whole), since God's character bears on one's own character (attitudes and dispositions) as much as on one's actions. For Jesus, we have a duty to be virtuous before God, on account of God's nature. "Be perfect, therefore, as your heavenly Father is perfect" (Matthew 5:48). Moreover, Jesus criticized external actions which, while in keeping with moral duty, lacked the proper motivations and aims. Those who gave large sums of money to the temple—which is a good thing—still lacked the virtue of the poor widow who gave only a fraction of a penny (Mark 12:41-44).

The master command of Jesus' ethics is love of God and love of others. In this, our duty lies. This penetrates to the essence of the entire moral law revealed in the Hebrew Scriptures and corresponds to the structure of the Ten Commandments, where the first four commands relate to God and the remaining six commands relate to others (Exodus 20:1-17; see also Deuteronomy 6:4). When asked, "Teacher, which is the greatest commandment in the Law?" Jesus replies:

"Love the Lord your God with all your heart and with all your soul and with all your mind." This is the first and greatest commandment. And the second is like it: "Love your neighbor as yourself." All the Law and the Prophets hang on these two commands (Matthew 22:37-40).

Jesus views God as worthy of love because of God's general concern for creation (Matthew 6:25-30) and because God sent his Son to redeem the world (John 3:16). This love implicates the innermost being—heart, soul, and mind—and ought to issue forth in external actions. Jesus speaks of fruit-bearing in this connection. The bad tree bears bad fruit and can do no other. The good tree, on the other hand, must bear good fruit (Matthew 7:16-18).

Jesus presents what came to be called "the golden rule" as another broad and affirmative ethical principle. "In everything, do to others what you would have them do to you, for this sums up the Law and the Prophets" (Matthew 7:12). This imperative is similar to the command found in the Jewish law to love one's neighbor as oneself (Leviticus 19:18). Negative formulations of a similar universal principle—don't do to others what you don't want them to do to you— appear in the literature of antiquity, but Jesus' construction is positive and altruistic, rather than cautious or restrictive; it is outgoing instead of defensive. A strong sense of compassion and sympathy is presupposed in this command; it requires "a reflective benevolence in which one finds ethical guidance in the imaginative placing of oneself in the position of another."[11] It jolts one out of self-absorption and widens the field of ethical awareness. Jesus' principle is not a mechanical formula but a summons to love and esteem others as unique and irreducible centers of worth and meaning.

The love Jesus commends is nothing less than extraordinary. He calls for love of one's enemies and prayer on their behalf. It is normal to love those who love us (though we often fail to do even that), but Jesus expects more. Instead of retaliation, one should turn the other cheek. Instead of begrudging one who forces you to go one mile, go the second mile (Matthew 5:38-48).

Christians have long debated whether these injunctions demand an absolute pacifism or whether Jesus addresses primarily interpersonal relationships and not matters of the state, where violence may sometimes be required to maintain order (as the Apostle Paul argues in Romans 13:1-7). In any event, the call to be a "peacemaker" (Matthew 5:9) is a radical and difficult one indeed. Jesus' nonviolent principles inspired and guided Martin Luther King, Jr., in his nonviolent approach to civil rights reform in the 1960s. Jesus also teaches his disciples that the revolutionary obligations of love can only be fulfilled through a dependence upon the spiritual power of Jesus himself, who is "the true vine" and the source of good ethical and spiritual fruit in his followers (John 15:1-17). This is where one encounters the "strength to love," as King entitled a book of his sermons.[12]

Jesus endorses heterosexual and monogamous marriage and the blessings of children as God's original and normative pattern for the full expression of human sexuality (Matthew 19:1-12; Mark 10:1-16; see Genesis 1-2). His views on divorce—stricter than many of his contemporaries—made women less subject to rejection by their husbands. However, he also values singleness as a gift from God for some, and does not see it as a curse (Matthew 19:10-12). He himself was unmarried, unlike most other rabbis at that time.

Jesus made several hyperbolic statements (which were common among rabbis of that day) to the effect that one's love for family should seem like hate compared to one's supreme love for God (Luke 14:26). Jesus also warned that allegiance to his cause would sometimes bring divisions within one's family. He did not advocate "peace at any price" when it came to fidelity to God's kingdom. Although he blessed the peacemakers, he did not advocate sacrificing one's commitment to the truth of his teachings (Matthew 10:32-39).

Jesus was not so other-worldly as to avoid teaching about material possessions and money. He spoke of this often and insistently. Many of his parables concern the use of material possessions. One should store up treasures in heaven rather than amassing the corruptible possessions of earth. No one can serve both God and money (Matthew 6:19-24). Jesus warned of the greedy accumulation of wealth because of its selfishness, injustice, and soul-numbing effects. "Watch out! Be on your guard against all kinds of greed; life does not consist in the abundance of possessions." He then told a parable of a man who trusted in wealth and not in God, who was called to account for his imbalanced priorities when God demanded his life from him (Luke 12:13-21; see also Luke 16:19-31). Jesus' penetrating question is often cited: "What good is it for you to gain the whole world, yet forfeit your soul?" (Mark 8:36). In a dialogue with a wealthy young man about God's requirement, Jesus looked on him with love and said he lacked one thing. "Go, sell everything you have and give to the poor, and you will have treasure in heaven. Then come, follow me" (Mark 10:21). The man demurred and left in sorrow, causing Jesus to remark that it is difficult for the rich to enter the kingdom of God. Nonetheless, "all things are possible with God" (Mark 10:27). Giving all one's possessions to the poor is not a universal command for all followers of Jesus (he did not present it as such), but it is illustrative of the willingness a disciple of Jesus should display in following him at all costs.

Jesus showed a special concern for the poor. Early in his ministry he declared:

> The Spirit of the Lord is on me, because he has anointed me to preach good news to the poor. He has sent me to proclaim freedom for the prisoners and recovery of sight for the blind, to release the oppressed, to proclaim the year of the Lord's favor (Luke 4:18-19).

Jesus' concern for the poor supports the importance of social action and reform; but his approach was not that of a political revolutionary, such as the Zealots of his day who wanted to overthrow Roman rule by force. In Jesus' day, unlike our own, political reform through popular participation was nearly impossible. Jesus did not intend to address social injustice by becoming a figure of political power. When his followers sought to make him king, he refused (John 6:15). However, the ethics of Jesus toward the poor has motivated great philanthropic and charitable work throughout history, as is evident in the actions of the early church (Acts 4:32; Galatians 2:10).

Jesus provoked people to attend to "the more important matters of the law," which are justice, mercy and faithfulness—moral concerns that have clear social implications for how one treats one's neighbor (Matthew 23:23). Jesus' statement that one must "give to Caesar what is Caesar's and to God what is God's" (Matthew 22:21) puts Caesar in his place under God without any anarchistic implications. His followers are to pay taxes, but not to emulate the dominating ways of political rulers (Luke 22:25-27). When warned that he should flee Herod's murderous intentions, Jesus was not intimidated: "Go tell that fox, 'I will drive out demons and heal people today and tomorrow, and on the third day I will reach my goal'" (Luke 13:32). The term "fox" in antiquity did not necessarily mean sly, but it definitely had pejorative implications of being treacherous, slanderous, and unprincipled. Jesus was clearly not cowed by political pressures, but neither did he foment a violent revolution.

Jesus' understanding of moral duties in relationship to the law of Israel is much debated, but a few comments are in order. First, he does not annul or criticize the law, but appeals to it as authoritative

(Matthew 5:17-20; John 10:35). He often quotes it as part of his argumentation. However, he regularly disputes the received interpretations of the law, especially concerning the Sabbath. Jesus accuses the religious establishment of making the law void through the additions of merely human and legalistic traditions. When challenged by the Pharisees and teachers of the law as to why he and his disciples did not follow "the traditions of the elders" (because they did not ritually wash their hands before eating), he changes the subject from the trivial to the profound. He exposes their practice of receiving money from children for religious purposes when this money rightly belonged to their parents. The command from the Ten Commandments, "Honor your father and your mother" (Exodus 20:12), was being violated by a false casuistry that benefited a religious institution at the expense of deeper family obligations (Matthew 15:1-9). Jesus flatly condemns this.

Jesus does not denigrate the law, but both deepens its demands and points beyond the law to a personal transformation based on faith in God's grace and provision for wayward humans. The rich young man mentioned above was told that he should keep the commandments, but the law was not enough.[13] He must follow Jesus, which for him meant selling his possessions and giving to the poor (Mark 10:17-31). One of Jesus' parables reveals that those who admit their shortcomings before God are in the right and those who think they are right before God because of their good works are in the wrong.

> To some who were confident of their own righteousness and looked down on everyone else, Jesus told this parable: "Two men went up to the temple to pray, one a Pharisee and the other a tax collector. The Pharisee stood up and prayed about himself: 'God, I thank you that I am not like other people—robbers, evildoers, adulterers—or even like this tax collector. I fast twice a week and give a tenth of all I get.' But the tax collector stood at a distance. He would not even look up to heaven, but beat his breast and said, 'God, have mercy on me, a sinner.' I tell you that this man, rather than the other, went home justified before God. For all who exalt themselves will be humbled, and those who humble themselves will be exalted" (Luke 18:9-14).

In four different encounters, Jesus commends people for faith that goes beyond the law by saying to those who trusted in him: "Your faith has healed (or saved) you" (Mark 5:21-34; 10:46-52; Luke 7:36-

50; 17:11-19). This means that their existential orientation toward Jesus—and not simply their adherence to religious law—brought them physical and spiritual restoration. The parable of the unworthy servants, which comes after a discussion of the need for faith, also indicates the insufficiency of mere duty (Luke 17:7-10). The reverent and trusting attitude displayed by one of the two criminals crucified with Jesus warranted this response from Jesus: "I tell you the truth, today you will be with me in paradise" (Luke 23:32-43). Jesus speaks of God's kingdom as a gift to be received, but one that should be sought after with proper faith (Luke 12:27-32). The escape from destruction and entrance into eternal life, according to Jesus, is found through belief in God's one and only Son (John 3:16-18). When asked, "What must we do to do the works God requires?" Jesus answered, "The work of God is this: to believe in the one he has sent" (John 6:29).

Consequences

Jesus was not a utilitarian. He did not make the experience of pleasure the measure of moral value, nor did he deem the maximizing of these states as ethically ideal. Rather, love of God, faith in God, the blessed life, and demonstrable and extraordinary love for others were the immovable pillars of his ethical thought. This meant there were duties to follow and virtues to exhibit. Nonetheless, Jesus did not ignore the consequential dimension of ethics. Dutiful, virtuous, and faithful people ought to bring about morally good states of affairs as much as possible.

Although Jesus reckons inner states as good or bad in themselves, he also identifies inward states as the engines of outward actions. "Good people bring good things out of the good stored up in their hearts, and evil people bring evil things out of the evil stored up in their hearts" (Luke 6:45). In the parable of the sheep and goats, Jesus commends those who have helped the downtrodden as those who authentically served him. He condemns those who have ignored the downtrodden by claiming they were in fact ignoring him (Matthew 25:31-46). He emphasizes the consequences of one's ultimate commitment. Jesus says, "This is to my Father's glory, that you bear much fruit, showing yourselves to be my disciples" (John 15:8). On the other hand, Jesus warns his followers against pretentiously parading their good deeds in order to impress others. Prayer, fasting, and giving should be done before God in secret, and not to elicit the approval of other people (Matthew 6:1-18).

Jesus also instructs his disciples to bring his message to their immediate environment and even to the entire world in order to find followers (Matthew 28:18-20; Acts 1:1-11). Given Jesus' own example and his teachings on virtue and duty, such activities ought not involve any deception, coercion, or manipulation. It is not enough simply to accept Jesus' way and savor it in isolation from the greater world. Love of neighbor and even love of one's enemy drives Jesus' adherents to broadcast and live out his message. For Jesus, love is an observable consequence of following him: "By this everyone will know that you are my disciples, if you love one another" (John 13:35).

Was Jesus' Ethic Too Restricted?

Some object that Jesus' teaching was not sufficiently broad or clear to be of relevance today. But the Christian tradition does not limit its ethics to Jesus' teaching; it also includes the Hebrew Scriptures that Jesus revered, as well as the rest of the New Testament. One could also argue that Jesus' principles and personal example are applicable to all the categories of ethical life, even if they do not supply specific rules for every possible situation. This lack of detailed rules is not incidental, however, since Jesus rejected the overly scrupulous orientation—legalism—of some of the religious leaders of his day. What is nonnegotiable and always applicable to every moral practice and decision is the love of God for us and our love for God and others.

Martin points out that Jesus did not condemn the institution of slavery, an omission he takes to be damning.[14] One cannot find a specific indictment of slavery in the Gospels—nor in any other literature of the world at that time. But an omission of condemnation is not the same as an endorsement of an institution's perpetual and cross-cultural legitimacy. The Gospels do not portray Jesus primarily as a social reformer who directly challenged all illegitimate authority. His mission was more focused than that. However, his instruction that his followers not lord it over others, but prize servanthood and humility instead, sets in motion an ethic ultimately incompatible with slavery (Mark 9:35). The Apostle Paul sees this when he deems slave traders to be sinful and under the condemnation of God's law (1 Timothy 1:9-11).

Similarly, Jesus does not directly speak about abortion, although he does show a high regard for children and sympathetically warns of a time when pregnant women will be in great danger (Matthew 24:15-20). However, the practice of abortion was condemned in both Jewish law and custom. The first-century Christian document called the

Didache condemned abortion and infanticide: "Thou shalt not murder a child by abortion nor kill them when born." Early Christians in the Roman Empire not only opposed abortion but rescued exposed infants, usually baby girls, from certain death.[15]

Jesus' worldview and mission were much broader than the dissection of ethical questions. However, Jesus possessed strong moral convictions and communicated them fervently and frequently. He called people to a life of comprehensive love evidenced by inner virtues, objective duties, and outward actions done in service to God and one's neighbor. Yet Jesus never made morality into a religion in itself, as one might argue Kant had done. Rather, for Jesus, the moral life is the proper response to God's loving and just principles and provisions.

---

[1] Craig Blomberg, *Jesus and the Gospels* (Nashville: Broadman and Holman, 1997), 384.

[2] Iris Murdoch, *The Sovereignty of the Good* (New York: Routledge and Kegan Paul, 1970).

[3] Michael Martin, *The Case Against Christianity* (Philadelphia: Temple University Press, 1990), 169.

[4] Martin, 170.

[5] Ibid., 170-171.

[6] Ibid., 170.

[7] Ibid.

[8] See Scott Rae, *Moral Choices*, 2nd ed. (Grand Rapids, MI: Zondervan Publishers, 2000), 99-100. For arguments against utilitarianism, see Rae, 84-88.

[9] Roger Scruton, *An Intelligent Person's Guide to Philosophy* (New York: Penguin Press, 1998), 138.

[10] Ibid.

[11] Harold B. Kuhn, "Golden Rule," in Carl F. H. Henry, ed., *Baker's Dictionary of Christian Ethics* (Baker Book House Company, 1973), 267.

[12] Martin Luther King, Jr., *The Strength to Love* (New York: Harper & Row, 1963).

[13] See Humphrey Carpenter, *Jesus*, in *Founders of Faith* (New York: Oxford University Press, 1986), 224-241; and Blomberg, 392-396.

[14] Martin, 168.

[15] See Michael J. Gorman, *Abortion and the Early Church* (Eugene, OR: Wifp and Stock Publishers, 1998).

7

Jesus' View of Women

World religions have been charged with not only permitting but perpetuating engrained patterns of sexism, patriarchy, and misogyny. These religions, it seems, must either change or be left behind by all who believe that women and men are equal in their rights, abilities, and potential. Some charge that Christianity demeans and marginalizes women, that it is a male religion in which men are given the preponderance of power, prestige, and influence. But what did the founder of Christianity teach about women?

Jesus and Women's Dignity

In the ancient context of Jesus' day, women typically had little social or cultural influence. Their roles were usually limited to domestic life, and in the home and family they had very little control over money or possessions apart from their fathers or husbands. A Jewish man would pray three benedictions each day, one of which thanked God for not making him a woman, although nothing like this is contained in the Hebrew Scriptures. Although they were written within and for patriarchial cultures, the Hebrew Scriptures present several women as leaders worthy of respect, especially Deborah, who was a prophet and judge over Israel (Judges 4-5). Other women, such as Miriam, Huldah, and Esther, play important roles as well. Although some women in ancient Judaism enjoyed some opportunities for leadership and respect, this was more the exception than the rule.[1] Within this cultural context, Jesus' respectful regard for women was unusual and sometimes even scandalous to those around him.

Although the New Testament is often assailed for being sexist and patriarchal, it fares far better than other ancient documents.

Consider Gnosticism. Elaine Pagels champions the Gnostics as proto-feminists who had a higher regard for women than writers of the New Testament.[2] This conclusion is quite speculative and probably based on spotty evidence and selective quotation.[3] The last saying of the Gnostic Gospel of Thomas expresses contempt for women:

> Simon Peter said to them, "Let Mary leave us, for women are not worthy of life." Jesus said, "I myself shall lead her in order to make her male, so that she too may become a living spirit resembling you males. For every woman who will make herself male will enter the kingdom of heaven."[4]

Spiritual gender switching is not required for the sake of Jesus' kingdom. Philip Jenkins's comment is apt: "Though women play so crucial a role in Gnostic texts, the religious system as a whole had nothing good to say of women."[5] Women were held in low esteem because of their close connection with physical procreation, which the dualistic Gnostics detested.

Men of Jesus' day typically viewed women's seductive behavior as responsible for most (if not all) sexual sin.[6] Jesus never did so. While he never condoned immodesty, Jesus judged sexual lust as a man's individual responsibility: "Anyone who looks at a woman lustfully has already committed adultery with her in his heart" (Matthew 5:28). Further, Jesus tightened the restrictions on divorce, not permitting men to divorce their wives for frivolous reasons (Matthew 5:31-32; 19:1-12), which, in a patriarchial setting, would leave women as vulnerable and outcast. While the consensus was that only women could commit adultery against their husbands, Jesus insisted that a husband could commit adultery against his wife; it was a sin for both sexes.

Jesus startled his hearers by proclaiming to the religious establishment that reformed prostitutes will enter the kingdom of God before they.

> I tell you the truth, the tax collectors and the prostitutes are entering the kingdom of God ahead of you. For John [the Baptist] came to you to show you the way of righteousness, and you did not believe him, but the tax collectors and the prostitutes did. And even after you saw this, you did not repent and believe him (Matthew 21:31-32).

Jesus identified the two most despised kinds of people and claimed that their repentance and faith would make them heirs of God's kingdom. On several occasions, prostitutes, the most scorned of women, received Jesus' commendation—not for their way of living, but because of their response to God's message through Jesus. They found hope in this remarkable man.

A woman who was called "a sinner" (someone guilty of a serious and scandalous sexual sin) anointed and kissed Jesus' feet while weeping. This occurred in the home of Simon, a Pharisee. Jesus accepted her actions as demonstrating her gratitude and love, and announced that her many sins had been forgiven. "Your faith has saved you; go in peace" (Luke 7:50).

Jesus showed compassion for women by healing them of various illnesses. He evidenced his willingness to disregard social and religious customs by not objecting to being touched by a woman who pressed through a crowd to reach out to him. Jesus healed her of a twelve-year flow of blood (Matthew 9:18), a malady that would have made her ritually "unclean," and thus untouchable according to levitical law. After healing another woman, who had been crippled for eighteen years, Jesus referred to her as "a daughter of Abraham." This showed respect and commendation, since Abraham was the father of the Jewish faith. "Son of Abraham" was common, "daughter of Abraham" was not; but Jesus affirmed her claim to Abraham's religious heritage. Jesus also healed various other women, including Peter's mother-in-law (Matthew 8:14-17) and the daughter of Jairus (Luke 8:40-56).

Jesus referred to women as worthy examples in many of his teachings. When he watched people deposit their gifts into the temple treasury, he saw the wealthy contribute large amounts, but was most impressed by a poor widow. "I tell you the truth, this poor widow has put more into the treasury than all the others" (Mark 12:41-44). In Luke chapter 15, Jesus tells three parables about God's rejoicing over repentance. There is the good shepherd who finds the lost sheep and the father who receives back his prodigal son. He also says this:

> Or suppose a woman has ten silver coins and loses one. Does she not light a lamp, sweep the house and search carefully until she finds it? And when she finds it, she calls her friends and neighbors together and says, "Rejoice with me; I have found my lost coin." In the same way, I tell you, there is rejoicing in the presence of the angels of God over one sinner who repents (Luke 15:8-10).

In another parable, Jesus lauds the persistence of the widow who implores an unjust judge for justice in her cause (Luke 18:1-8). Millard

Erickson notes that "in all these instances, Jesus tacitly shows that a woman can represent the activity of God or a righteous individual equally well as can a man."[7] Jesus shows no gender favoritism in his examples of praiseworthy behavior. Other parables speak of foolish women and men as well (Matthew 24:40-41; Luke 17:34-35). Although Jesus tells his disciples to pray to "Our Father" (Matthew 6:9), the teachings discussed above—along with other teachings in the Scriptures—show that he is speaking of God metaphorically, not of a gendered male being.[8]

While decrying the spiritual obliviousness of one of his audiences, Jesus said that at the final judgment two witnesses would be brought forth against them: those who repented at the preaching of Jonah, and an ancient Gentile woman. "The Queen of the South will rise at the judgment with this generation and condemn it; for she came from the ends of the earth to listen to Solomon's wisdom, and now one greater than Solomon is here" (Matthew 12:42). This reference to the Queen of Sheba was remarkable because at that time rabbis did not typically accept the legal testimony of a woman. Yet Jesus predicted that her word—against that of the male religious authorities—would be determinative in the final scheme of things. Jesus, the "one greater than Solomon," sides with her against the male religious elite. This was unheard of in his day.

Jesus did not annul family relationships, but he refused to endorse the common idea that women exist solely to be mothers and wives in the home. After Jesus gave a lesson about evil spirits, a woman from the crowd called out, "Blessed is the mother who gave you birth and nursed you." Jesus replied, "Blessed rather are those who hear the word of God and obey it" (Luke 11:27-28). Instead of reinforcing the idea that motherhood is the primary or overriding purpose of women, Jesus put more value on being attentive and obedient to God's word. This is an implicit endorsement of the right of women to be taught, which was not usually permitted in Jewish circles.

Women and Theological Instruction

Jesus' affirmation of women as students of religious instruction is made more clear in the account of the sisters Mary and Martha, close associates of Jesus. After inviting Jesus and his disciples into their home, Mary sat at Jesus' feet listening to his teaching. Martha was distracted by all her chores of hospitality and said to Jesus, "Lord, don't you care that my sister has left me to do the work by myself? Tell her to help me!" Jesus replied, "Martha, Martha, you are worried and upset about many things, but only one thing is needed. Mary has chosen what is better, and it will not be taken away from her" (Luke 10:38-42). Jesus does more than tell Martha not to be so hyperactive. He endorses Mary's right to be taught, remarking that this is more important than the traditional province of a woman (preoccupation with domestic tasks).

In the account of the death of Martha's brother, Lazarus, the same woman that Jesus had corrected for not listening to his teaching now affirms a vivid theological doctrine about him. In a discussion with Jesus about life, death, and resurrection, Martha makes a declaration very similar to the one given by the Apostle Peter (Matthew 16:16). She says, "I believe that you are the Christ, the Son of God, who was to come into the world" (John 11:27). She thus gives one of the strongest statements of messianic faith in the Gospels, and so becomes a model of theological veracity concerning Jesus.

Jesus' willingness to interact without condescension with women, even the outcasts, is obvious in his encounter and long dialogue with the Samaritan woman at Jacob's well in Sychar (John 4:5-42). Fatigued from the journey, Jesus asks a woman, who had come to draw water, if she would give him a drink. The woman was stunned since she recognized him as a Jew, and Jews had nothing to do with Samaritans. The Jews held that Samaritans were "unclean," and that a Jew would become unclean by touching a vessel handled by a Samaritan. Jesus uses the opportunity to discuss his mission. "If you knew the gift of God and who it is that asks you for a drink, you would have asked him and he would have given you living water." The woman is puzzled by this, and wonders how Jesus could provide this, since he had nothing with which to draw the water. Jesus responds, "All who drink this water will be thirsty again, but those who drink the water I give them will never thirst. Indeed, the water I give them will become in them a spring of water welling up to eternal life."

The woman requests this water of Jesus, but Jesus says that she should call her husband and then come back. She replies that she has no husband. Jesus says that she has had five husbands and that the man she now has is not her husband. The woman, who must have been startled by the knowledge displayed by this Jewish stranger, declares that he is a prophet. She then says, "Our ancestors worshipped on this mountain, but you Jews claim that the place where we must worship is in Jerusalem." To this Jesus offers a theological explanation and a prophecy.

Believe me, woman, a time is coming when you will worship the Father neither on this mountain nor in Jerusalem. You Samaritans worship what you do not know; we worship what we do know, for salvation is from the Jews. Yet a time is coming and has now come when the true worshippers will worship the Father in spirit and truth, for they are the kind of worshippers the Father seeks. God is spirit, and his worshippers must worship in spirit and in truth.

The woman returns the theological volley and confesses: "'I know that Messiah' (called Christ) 'is coming. When he comes, he will explain everything to us.' Jesus then declares, "I who speak to you am he." This is the only time in the Gospels, prior to his trial and crucifixion (Matthew 26:62-65), when Jesus directly claims to be the Messiah. He says it during a theological conversation with a Samaritan woman. It is no wonder that John tells us that when "his disciples returned and were surprised to find him talking with a woman." The woman then went to her town and proclaimed, "Come, see a man who told me everything I ever did. Could this be the Christ?" At her urging, many Samaritans came to Jesus. They convinced him to stay with them for two days, during which they heard his teachings. Many became believers. A social outcast of the oppressed gender was authorized by Jesus to tell others about him. He did not require a man to do it. Jesus' theological discussions with women were remarkable because Jewish males would not discuss such things with women. Jesus, however, deemed both women and men worthy and qualified to converse on God's ways with the human race.

Why No Women Apostles?

Despite these accounts of Jesus' teachings and actions regarding women, some still protest that he was not truly affirming and welcoming of women because he did not select any women to be apostles. Therefore, he did not see them as worthy of religious leadership. Several considerations mitigate this charge that he excluded women because he had a low view of them.

First, males dominated and outranked females in Jesus' day to a degree we can barely imagine. Society was hierarchical in the spheres of state, religion, and the household. In the face of this, Jesus frequently underscored the virtue of humble service.

The kings of the Gentiles lord it over them; and those who exercise authority over them call themselves Benefactors. But you are not to be like that. Instead, the greatest among you should be like the youngest, and the one who rules like the one who serves. For who is greater, the one who is at the table or the one who serves? Is it not the one who is at the table? But I am among you as one who serves (Luke 22:25-27).

Such a radical pattern of humility and service would not allow for male exploitation of women. Jesus' denunciation of those who preyed on defenseless widows was consistent with this countercultural stance (Mark 12:38-40).

Second, the Gospels report that women were among his close followers. Martha and Mary have already been mentioned. A group of women—Mary Magdalene, Joanna, Susanna and others—listened to Jesus and traveled with Jesus and his male disciples. "These women were helping to support them out of their own means" (Luke 8:1-3). The faithfulness of Jesus' female disciples was most notable during the last days of his ministry. Unlike most of the male disciples, the women who followed Jesus were at the crucifixion (Matthew 27:55-56). Jesus' burial was witnessed by at least two women, Mary Magdalene and "the other Mary" (Matthew 27:61). All four Gospels report that women—including Mary Magdalene, "the other Mary," and Salome—were the first to discover the empty tomb and to proclaim Jesus' resurrection to the initially unbelieving male disciples.[9]

Third, given the highly patriarchial setting of Jesus' ministry, it would have been unlikely if not culturally impossible for him to have ministered effectively with women in his innermost circle. As David Scholer notes: "It is remarkable and significant enough that women, at least eight of whom are known by name and often with as much or more data as some of the Twelve, were included as disciples and proclaimers during Jesus ministry."[10] Scholer also observes that the original Jewish apostles did not continue to serve as the models for church leadership after the earliest days of the church at Jerusalem. Faithful Gentiles could be leaders, as well. Moreover, despite a few local restrictions on women in some settings, there is evidence of women serving in leadership during the New Testament period.[11]

In light of Jesus' words and deeds, novelist and philosopher Dorothy L. Sayers's comments deserve full quotation.

Perhaps it is no wonder that women were first at the Cradle and last at the Cross. They had never known a man like this Man—there never has been such another. A prophet and teacher who never nagged them, never flattered or coaxed or patronized; who never made jokes about them, never treated them either as "the women, "God help us!" or "The Ladies, God bless them!"; who rebuked without querulousness and praised without condescension; who took their questions and arguments seriously; who never mapped out their sphere for them, never urged them to be feminine or jeered at them for being female; who had no ax to grind and no uneasy male dignity to defend; who took them as he found them and was completely unself-conscious. There is no act, no sermon, no parable in the Gospel that borrows its pungency from female perversity; nobody could possibly guess from the words and deeds of Jesus that there was anything "funny" about woman's nature.[12]

---

[1] David Scholer, "Women" in *Dictionary of Jesus and the Gospels*, ed. Joel B. Green, Scot McKnight, I. Howard Marshall (Downers Grove, IL: InterVarsity Press, 1992), 880-881.

[2] Elaine Pagels, *The Gnostic Gospels* (New York: Random House, 1979), 48-69.

[3] See Kathleen McVey, "Gnosticism, Feminism and Elaine Pagels," *Theology Today*, January 1981, 498-501.

[4] *Gospel of Thomas*, saying 114.

[5] Philip Jenkins, *Hidden Gospels: How the Search for Jesus Lost Its Way* (New York: Oxford University Press, 2001), 211.

[6] Scholer, 880.

[7] Millard Erickson, *The Word Made Flesh: An Incarnational Christology* (Grand Rapids, MI: Baker Book House, 1992), 582.

[8] See Rebecca Merrill Groothuis, *Good News for Women: A Biblical Picture of Gender Equality* (Grand Rapids, MI: Baker Books, 1997), chapter four.

[9] Matthew 28:1-8; Mark 16:1-8; Luke 24:1-11; John 20:1-10.

[10] Scholer, 886.

[11] See Linda Belleville, *Women Leaders and the Church: Three Crucial Questions* (Grand Rapids, MI: Baker Books, 2000), 39-69, and R. M. Groothuis, chapters 5-10.

[12] Dorothy L. Sayers, *Are Women Human?* (Grand Rapids, MI: Eerdmans, 1971), 47.

8

"Who Do You Say That I Am?"

The identity of Jesus—and not merely the truth or rationality of his teachings—has been a source of perennial debate. He himself sparked this debate in a number of ways. The student of Kant may ask whether his "Copernican revolution" in epistemology is a rational way to handle the challenge of Hume's skepticism, but will not ask whether Kant was divine or even a prophet or mystic. The same is true for nearly all of the great thinkers in the Wadsworth Philosophers Series, with the exception of Sidhartha Guatama, whose purported identity as "the awakened one" (the Buddha) is a matter of considerable import.[1]

A great deal of the controversy Jesus ignited centered on statements and actions which directly or indirectly raised the question of his identity, as we have already seen in earlier chapters. Jesus sometimes put the question directly. At Caesarea Philippi, Jesus asked his disciples what people were saying about the Son of Man. They answered, "Some say John the Baptist; others say Elijah; and still others, Jeremiah or one of the prophets." Jesus pressed, "Who do you say I am?" Peter replied, "You are the Christ, the Son of the living God." Jesus commends Peter and claims that it was revealed to him not "by flesh and blood, but by my Father in heaven." This was a confession that Jesus was the Messiah, the promised One of Israel. Jesus took this confession to be so pivotal to the life of his movement that he declared, "And I tell you that you are Peter, and on this rock I will build my church, and the gates of hell will not overcome it" (Matthew 16:13-18).

How one assesses the identity of Jesus in light of narratives such as the above depends greatly on one's historical assessment of the Gospels. Many scholars have deconstructed the traditional Christian view of Jesus as the divine Messiah and reconstructed a host of various alternatives based on what they take to be factual in the Gospels. The Jesus Seminar finds very little in the Gospels that is rooted in the historical Jesus, and the few sayings it certifies tend to be pithy aphorisms and not the more theologically involved teachings. I addressed some of this debate in chapter two, where I argued for the essential reliability of the Gospels. Here I will present the Gospel materials and other New Testament writings that relate to Jesus' identity. I will then take up a few of the philosophical questions raised by the Gospel portrait of Jesus.

Jesus on Jesus

Jesus was undoubtedly a theist, but his belief went beyond a mere metaphysical claim. Jesus professed to have a unique knowledge of God. In a passage widely regarded as authentic even by many generally skeptical of much in the Gospels, Jesus says:

> All things have been committed to me by my Father. No-one knows the Son except the Father, and no-one knows the Father except the Son and those to whom the Son chooses to reveal him (Matthew 11:27).

Jesus says that "all things" have been given to him by God. No prophet, priest, king, angel, or anyone else in the Hebrew Scriptures made this claim. Jesus establishes a unique and exclusive relationship between himself—as *the* Son," not merely "*a* son"—and "the Father." He also equates the Father's knowledge of the Son with the Son's knowledge of the Father. This implies an equality of divine knowledge. Further, Jesus claims unique ability as the absolute and exclusive revelator of the Father and as mediator between the Father and those who receive the revelation of the Father through the Son.

Jesus' statement about the Son's singular relationship to the Father closely parallels many claims in the Gospel of John, particularly his controversial answer to Thomas' question, "Lord, we don't know where you are going, so how can we know the way?"

Jesus answered, "I am the way and the truth and the life. No-one comes to the Father except through me. If you really knew me, you would know my Father as well. From now on , you do know him and have seen him" (John 14:5-7; see also John 1:18).

As in Matthew 11:27, Jesus claims be the unique and exclusive mediator between humans and God the Father, and to be the unique and exclusive revelation of God to humans. To know Jesus is to know the Father as well. Not to know Jesus is not to know the Father. Jesus' singular role as mediator was an early item of attention and declaration in the early Christian movement. Peter preaches the same concept shortly after Jesus' death (Acts 4:12) and Paul also affirms it in his first letter to the young pastor Timothy (1 Timothy 2:5) in about AD 55.

Jesus' conception of God as his Father caused opposition because of its radical implications. Jesus said, "My Father is always at his work to this very day, and I, too, am working." In other words, his work is tantamount to God's work. John tells us that for this reason, the religious opposition to Jesus redoubled their efforts to kill him because they interpreted his words to mean that "he was even calling God his own Father, making himself equal with God." In Jesus' long response to this charge, he never denied the implication that he was putting himself on the same level as God himself (John 5:17-47).

The Gospels give no references to repentance, apology, or contrition in Jesus' life. Unlike the prophets before him and the apostles after, he displays no sense of personal guilt, shame, or regret. Hence, his relationship with God is pure and unobstructed. He claims to please his Father always (John 8:29). Yet, he does not appear to be a megalomaniac or egomaniac who refuses to admit wrong out of self-deception and/or conceit.

Jesus' sense of closeness with God also translates into his certainty, sense of mission, and authority. Although he is not an inhuman entity who floats above the ground dispensing heavenly memoranda, he never uses words indicating hesitancy, reservation, or perplexity about moral, philosophical, or theological matters. He utters challenging moral demands such as "love your enemies" (Matthew 5:44) without reservation. He issues grand promises without caution, such as, "Blessed are those who hunger and thirst for righteousness, for they will be filled" (Matthew 5:6) and, "If you hold to my teaching, you are really my disciples. Then you will know the truth, and the truth will set you free" (John 8:31-32). He resolutely affirms that "heaven and earth will pass away, but my words will never pass away" (Matthew 24:35). He even warns his hearers that their final destiny depends on their response to him (Mark 8:38). He declares that the kingdom of God is at hand and that if national Israel rejects his message, it would be left desolate because it would be rejecting God's very own invitation (Matthew 23:37-39).[2] Without tentativeness or qualification, Jesus summons people to give themselves to his cause:

> Those who would come after me must deny themselves and take up their cross and follow me. For those who want to save their lives will lose them, but those who lose their lives for me will find them (Matthew 16:24).

Jesus' sense of certainty also extends to claims about himself, which carry with them—if true—profound consequences. At a home in Capernaum, Jesus was teaching to a full house when a paralytic was lowered down through the roof into his midst. Jesus says to this man, "Son, your sins are forgiven," thus causing several teachers of the law to think, "Why does this fellow talk like that? He's blaspheming! Who can forgive sins but God alone?" Jesus replies:

> "Why are you thinking these things? Which is easier: to say to the paralytic, 'Your sins are forgiven,' or to say, 'Get up, take your mat and walk?' But that you may know that the Son of Man has authority on earth to forgive sins. . . ." He said to the paralytic, "I tell you, get up, take your mat and go home" (Mark 2:5-11).

The man was healed, and Jesus did not dispute the idea raised by his audience that only God could forgive sins. Instead, he offered his power to heal as a vindication and verification of his authority to forgive sins and so merit divine status. After a woman of ill repute displayed her devotion to him by anointing his head with oil, Jesus similarly pronounced the woman forgiven of her sins. "Who is this who even forgives sin?" the onlookers wondered. Jesus announced to her, "Your faith has saved you" (Luke 7:36-50).

C. S. Lewis points out that Jesus' claim to have the authority to forgive sins is theologically significant. It is not difficult to understand a person forgiving another for offenses against himself, such as theft or rudeness. You forgive the one who offended you. But what would one think of a man who "forgave you for treading on other men's toes and stealing other men's money?"

He told people that their sins were forgiven, and never waited to consult all the other people whom their sin had undoubtedly injured. He unhesitatingly behaved as if He was the party chiefly concerned, the person chiefly offended in all offences. This makes sense only if He really was the God whose laws are broken and whose love is wounded in every sin. In the mouth of any speaker who is not God, these words would imply what I can only regard as a silliness and conceit unrivalled by any other character in history.[3]

In a quarrel concerning Sabbath observance, Jesus concludes that, "The Sabbath was made for people, not people for the Sabbath." He then adds, "So the Son of Man is Lord even of the Sabbath" (Mark 2:27-28). The Jews believed that their Creator ordained the Sabbath and set down principles becoming of its sanctity (Genesis 2:1-3; Exodus 20:8-11). Therefore, God alone is Lord of the Sabbath. Yet Jesus claims to have the final jurisdiction over the Sabbath as its "Lord," not merely as its rabbinical interpreter or advocate. No prophet, priest, king commoner, or angel in the Hebrew Scriptures ever claimed to be "Lord even of the Sabbath." Jesus professes to have a divine authority; he is not merely offering an opinion on religion.

After Jesus is accused of being demon-possessed, he denies this, and claims that he honors his Father, that his Father glorifies him, and that "Your father Abraham rejoiced at the thought of seeing my day; he saw it and was glad." After this messianic claim, his opponents retort, "You are not fifty years old, and you have seen Abraham!" "I tell you the truth," Jesus answered, "before Abraham was born, I am!" At this they picked up stones to stone Jesus, but he escaped (John 8:48-59). Their attempt to stone Jesus was a response to blasphemy (see Leviticus 24:16). His statement is not only a claim to have existed during Abraham's day hundreds of years earlier (in that case he would have said, "Before Abraham was born, I was"); rather, it is a claim that Jesus existed as God during Abraham's time. The phrase "I am" harks back to God's self-revelation to Moses when he said, "I am that I am" (Exodus 3:14). Hence the violent response from Jesus' audience.

Many responded to Jesus' controversial claims and dramatic actions by believing in him. Some even worshiped him. We find Jesus receiving the spontaneous worship of his followers after he calmed the storm at sea (Matthew 14:33) and after his resurrection (Matthew 28:9,17). The disciple Thomas, who initially doubted Jesus' resurrection, later confessed to his face, "My Lord and my God!" (John

20:28). Jesus neither rejected nor corrected any of these acts of
obeisance.

Evaluating Jesus' Statements

We could multiply references to Jesus' sense of unique identity
and authority as indicated by his words and actions.[4] But these are
sufficient to show that the Gospel record does not present Jesus as
merely a prophet, a healer, an exorcist, a teacher of Scripture, or a
philosopher—although he was all these things. But if Jesus did make
staggering claims, what ought one make of him? There seem to be but
three alternatives. Assuming the historical accuracy of the Gospel
records, Jesus was either: (1) intentionally *deceiving* others (and an
entire later movement) about his identity. In this case he was a liar. Or
(2) he was *self-deceived*, thinking that he was God when he was not. In
this case he was a lunatic. Or (3) he was truthful in his claims and their
entailments. In this case Jesus was *divine*. This argument is famously
given (but not invented) by C. S. Lewis, and is sometimes called the
"trilemma"—liar, lunatic, or Lord. These are the three options for
Jesus' identity, none of which allows one to affirm rationally that he is
merely a good teacher, a moral exemplar, a prophet, or a mystic. Lewis
attempts to tighten the logical screws.

> A man who was merely a man and said the sort of things Jesus
> said would not be a great moral teacher. He would either be a
> lunatic—on the level with the man who says he is a poached
> egg—or else he would be the Devil of Hell. You must make
> your choice. Either this man was, and is, the Son of God: or else
> a madman or something worse. You can shut Him up for a fool,
> you can spit at Him and kill Him as a demon; or you can fall at
> His feet and call Him Lord and God. But let us not come with
> any patronising nonsense about His being a great human teacher.
> He has not left that open to us. He did not intend to. [5]

Stephen T. Davis, a contemporary analytical philosopher, has
developed this argument with analytic precision in "Was Jesus Mad,
Bad, or God?" I cannot do justice here to his careful argument, but I
leave it to the reader to think through its basic structure. Davis claims
that his argument establishes the rationality of belief in the Incarnation.

90

"Who Do You Say That I Am?"

1. Jesus claimed, either explicitly or implicitly, to be divine.
2. Jesus was either right or wrong in claiming to be divine.
3. If Jesus was wrong in claiming to be divine, Jesus was either mad or bad.
4. Jesus was not bad.
5. Jesus was not mad.
6. Therefore, Jesus was not wrong in claiming to be divine.
7. Therefore, Jesus was right in claiming to be divine.
8. Therefore, Jesus was divine.[6]

A philosophical challenge to Jesus as God Incarnate is given by those who claim that the notion of a being who is both divine and human (the orthodox claim) is either logically incoherent or meaningless.[7] If it is meaningless, it can be neither true nor false. This seems to be the weaker claim, since the statement, "Jesus possessed divine properties and human properties," does not read as a meaningless string of words, as does the statement, "Colorless green ideas sleep furiously." The former claim is intelligible, even if remarkable. The latter has no possible meaning or referent. But is the concept of the Incarnation coherent philosophically?

The case against the coherence of the Incarnation is that one being cannot possess both divine and human attributes (or a divine and a human nature), since these attributes are antithetical. To oversimplify somewhat, humans are finite and God is infinite. The infinite cannot be united in one being with the finite. Therefore, the idea of Jesus as equally God and human is false. It is as contradictory as a square circle.

Some Christian thinkers, such as Søren Kierkegaard in his *Philosophical Fragments*, have embraced the Incarnation as an irresolvable paradox. He called it "the absolute paradox," and a necessary offense to human reason. One holds to it by passionate faith, not because it is reasonable. A more intellectually engaging approach has been given by several Christian philosophers and theologians. Instead of reveling in paradox (or even absurdity), they attempt to erase the apparent contradiction while retaining a sense of mystery regarding Jesus as the God-man. This strategy conceptualizes ways in which Jesus' divine and human attributes could cohere in one person.

If the claim for the Incarnation means that Jesus possesses only divine attributes and only human attributes, the claim is contradictory and, therefore, necessarily false. An object cannot be completely and only spherical and completely and only square. But one may argue that Jesus possesses divine and human attributes in a coherent arrangement. Gordon Lewis and Bruce Demarest put it this way.

91

In a subcontrary relationship neither the affirmation nor the denial is universal, hence both may be true. For example… "Some of the attributes of a person are physical" and "Some of the attributes of a person are nonphysical." Similarly, "Some attributes of the person of Jesus Christ are divine and some are human." Neither the divine set of attributes nor the human set of attributes is said to be all that he has, and so neither affirmation is necessarily false.[8]

Christian thinkers (following the lead of the Apostle Paul in Philippians 2:5-11) have written of Jesus suspending the use of some of his divine attributes for the purpose of the Incarnation without ontologically losing these attributes. Michael Jordon might play a pick-up basketball game with some junior high children without using all of his abilities. He would continue to possess powers that were held in check for a reason. It suffices to say that this debate has generated some very sophisticated philosophical and theological perspectives that take seriously the charge that the Incarnation is logically incoherent.[9]

Crucifixion and Resurrection Claims

Prior to raising Lazarus from the dead, Jesus affirms that he is "the resurrection and the life" (John 11:25). Near the end of his ministry, Jesus predicts his execution in Jerusalem and that his death would not be that of a mere martyr, but that he would rise from the dead "on the third day" (Matthew 16:21-22; 20:18-19).

A disproportional percentage of the Gospel accounts address the last days of Jesus' life, leading up to his crucifixion. Jesus repeatedly speaks of giving his life for God's redemptive purposes. After emphasizing the importance of serving others, Jesus claims that "the Son of Man did not come to be served, but to serve, and to give his life as a ransom for many" (Matthew 20:28). Referring to himself, Jesus declares, "The good shepherd lays down his life for the sheep" (John 10:11).

Jesus and the New Testament writers identify Jesus as the suffering servant of the Book of Isaiah, the innocent one who is punished for the wrongdoings of others that they might know God's peace.[10] (Isaiah 53; Matthew 8:17; Luke 22:37; 1 Peter 2:24). Jesus underscores the importance of his death at the Last Supper, when he speaks of the bread as his body and the cup as "my blood of the covenant, which is poured out for many for the forgiveness of sins." Yet Jesus said he would drink the "fruit of the vine" again with his disciples in his Father's kingdom (Matthew 26:26-29). He would rise again.

Some see the resurrection of Jesus as a moot point, believing that his life and teachings are sufficient to enshrine him as one of the world's wisest and best people. Those who deny or doubt Jesus' resurrection certainly may benefit from some of his teachings and from his model. Nevertheless, the Jesus of the Gospels hung his destiny and identity on the resurrection. The earliest record of the Jesus movement (the Book of Acts) presents his disciples proclaiming the resurrection of their leader as the cornerstone of their faith and community. Every sermon in Acts centers on the resurrection and collapses without it. The Apostle Paul went so far as to say that "if Christ has not been raised, our preaching is useless and so is your faith" (1 Corinthians 15:14). Paul understood Jesus' resurrection to be the guarantee and requirement of the salvation and afterlife of believers. Yet he was confident that "Christ has indeed been raised from the dead" (1 Corinthians 15:20).

Some believers opt for fideism concerning Jesus' resurrection: there is no need for any historical or evidential support. Faith affirms it. Period. Notwithstanding, the resurrection has spawned vigorous academic debate over the centuries, and this shows no signs of letting up. Taking their lead from Paul, who appeals to numerous witnesses of the resurrected Jesus—some of whom were still living at the time of his writing in AD 50s (1 Corinthians 15:3-8)—many modern scholars believe there is good reason to esteem Jesus as no longer dead and buried but alive and resurrected. I cannot canvass the debate fully, but a few items stand out.

If one presupposes naturalism metaphysically, then one will rule out all miracles *a priori*. *Any* naturalistic explanation will trump *any* supernatural explanation; no evidence for the supernatural will even be considered. According to the *methodological* naturalist, miracles may occur, but the historian is never warranted in considering them historical.[11] But if one is a theist (or even an agnostic) and is open to the possibility of historical evidence for the supernatural, then Jesus' resurrection becomes a possibility. One must then consult the available evidence and give the best explanation for it, all things considered.

The positive case claims that Jesus' space-time and bodily resurrection best explains the New Testament testimony to this fact. Without the resurrection, the Gospels and the rest of the New Testament lose their vital center of reality, faith, hope, and love. As argued in chapter two, it is rational to believe that the Gospels were written by credible authors who would not likely manufacture falsehoods, particularly titanic falsehoods such as the resurrection of their decaying founder. The church's essential and ancient practices of the Lord's supper (1 Corinthians 11:17-34) and baptism (Romans 6:3, 4) presuppose Jesus' resurrection. Believing Jews also changed their day of worship from Saturday to Sunday, in honor of the resurrection (Acts 20:7). Although tomb veneration was common in Jesus' day, we have no evidence of Jesus' tomb being venerated. The best explanation for this is that the tomb was empty. Later a tradition developed that recognized the spot of Jesus' *empty* tomb, something very different from previous tomb veneration.[12] The Gospels report that women were the first witnesses of the risen Jesus. This is significant because women were generally taken to be untrustworthy as witnesses. If a writer were going to fabricate a resurrection appearance, he would not have included women. These accounts have the ring of authenticity. In discussing Christianity as a "resurrection movement," New Testament scholar and leading voice of the "third quest for the historical Jesus," N. T. Wright, puts it this way:

> There is no evidence for a form of early Christianity in which the resurrection was not a central belief. Nor was this belief, as it were, bolted on to Christianity at the edge. It was the central driving force, informing the whole movement.[13]

Contemporary philosopher and biblical scholar William Lane Craig has written extensively on the resurrection as a fact of history and has publicly debated several scholars who deny it. Craig bases his pro-resurrection arguments on four facts that he believes are well-established among a broad spectrum of New Testament scholars.

1. Jesus died from crucifixion and was buried by Joseph of Arimathea in his personal tomb.
2. On Sunday following the crucifixion, Jesus' tomb was found empty by women followers.
3. On many occasions and under various conditions, different people experienced appearances of Jesus alive from the dead.
4. The original disciples believed that Jesus was resurrected despite their expectations that the Messiah (Christ) would not die and be resurrected.[14]

Craig then argues that these facts are better accounted for by the resurrection of Jesus than by other hypotheses. A key figure of the Jesus Seminar, John Dominic Crosson, reconstructs the Gospel accounts and argues against Craig that Jesus died and was buried in a shallow grave—apart from any resurrection, which was an invention of the early church.[15] Gerd Lüdeman, who seems to reject miracles *a priori* as being part of a premodern (and irrational) mentality, develops the theory against Craig that the appearances of Jesus were hallucinations, not the actual appearances of a resurrected person.[16] It is interesting that the Jewish New Testament scholar Pinchas Lapide (who is not a Christian) finds the hallucination theory incredible:

> If the defeated and depressed group of disciples overnight could change into a victorious movement of faith, based only on autosuggestion or self-deception—without a fundamental faith experience—then this would be a much greater miracle than the resurrection itself.[17]

Critics point out that there are inconsistencies in the details of the resurrection appearances in the four Gospels. They use this as evidence for the falsity of the resurrection.[18] Other scholars argue that these inconsistencies are only apparent and do not falsify the fact of the resurrection. One finds a difference of perspective—not a collection of differing fictions—that indicates authenticity instead of collusion. All the accounts clearly agree on the factuality of Jesus' death, burial, and resurrection. Various scholars have synthesized the four reports into chronologically consistent narratives.[19]

The question of Jesus' identity, crucifixion, and resurrection is more than a matter of scholarly debate (upon which we have only briefly lighted). Because Jesus articulated a full-orbed worldview and often argued for it philosophically, our view of Jesus and his teachings also engenders questions about ourselves, our morality, our place in the cosmos, and the afterlife. But Jesus did not stop there. Through his words and deeds he presented himself—if the documents are to be accepted as factual—as the unique revelator and mediator of the ultimate and sacred reality, the hinge of history, and the portal to eternity.

---

[1] See Bart Gruzalski, *On the Buddha* (Belmont, CA: Wadsworth/Thomson Learning, 2000).

[2] See N. T. Wright, *The Challenge of Jesus: Discovering Who Jesus Was and Is* (Downers Grove, IL: InterVarsity Press, 1999), 48-52.

[3] C. S. Lewis, *Mere Christianity* (New York: MacMillan Publishing Company, 1996; orig. pub. 1943), 55.

[4] See Millard Erickson, *The Word Made Flesh: An Incarnational Christology* (Grand Rapids: Baker Books, 1992), 431-454.

[5] Lewis, 56.

[6] Stephen T. Davis, "Was Jesus Mad, Bad, or God?" in Stephen T. Davis, Daniel Kendall, and Gerald O'Collins, eds., *The Incarnation* (Oxford University Press, 2001), 221-245.

[7] John Hick, *The Metaphor of God Incarnate: Christology in a Pluralistic Age* (Louisville, KY: Westminster/John Knox Press, 1993).

[8] Gordon Lewis and Bruce Demarest, *Integrative Theology* (Grand Rapids, MI: Zondervan, 1992), 2:350.

[9] See Erickson on the metaphysics of the Incarnation, 507-576; and Thomas Senor, "The Incarnation and the Trinity," in Michael J. Murray, ed. *Reason for the Hope Within* (Grand Rapids, MI: Eerdmans, 1999), 238-253.

[10] See Isaiah 53; Matthew 8:17; Luke 22:37; 1 Peter 2:24; etc.

[11] See the discussion on miracles in chapter two.

[12] Jeff Sheler, *Is the Bible True?* (Grand Rapids, Zondervan, 1999), 225-226.

[13] Wright, 133.

[14] See William Lane Craig, "Opening Address," in *Will the Real Jesus Please Stand Up? A Debate Between William Lane Craig and John Dominic Crosson* (Grand Rapids, MI: Baker Books, 1998), 26-29.

[15] John Dominic Crosson, "Opening Remarks," in Ibid., 33-39.

[16] Gerd Lüdeman, "Opening Statement," in Paul Copan and Ronald Tacelli, *Jesus' Resurrection: Fact or Figment: A Debate Between William Lane Craig and Gerd Lüdeman* (Downers Grove, IL: InterVarsity Press, 2000), 40-45; see also 52-55; 60-62; 66-70; 149-161. See also Craig's responses to Lüdeman's claims.

[17] Pinchas Lapide, *The Resurrection of Jesus* (Minneapolis: Augsburg Publishing House, 1983), 126.

[18] See Michael Martin, *The Case Against Christianity* (Philadelphia: Temple University Press, 1991), 73-104.

[19] See Murray J. Harris, "A Suggested Harmonization of the Resurrection Narratives," *in Three Crucial Questions About Jesus* (Grand Rapids, MI: Baker Books, 1994), 107-109; and Craig L. Blomberg, *Jesus and The Gospels* (Nashville: Broadman and Holman, 1997), 354-360.